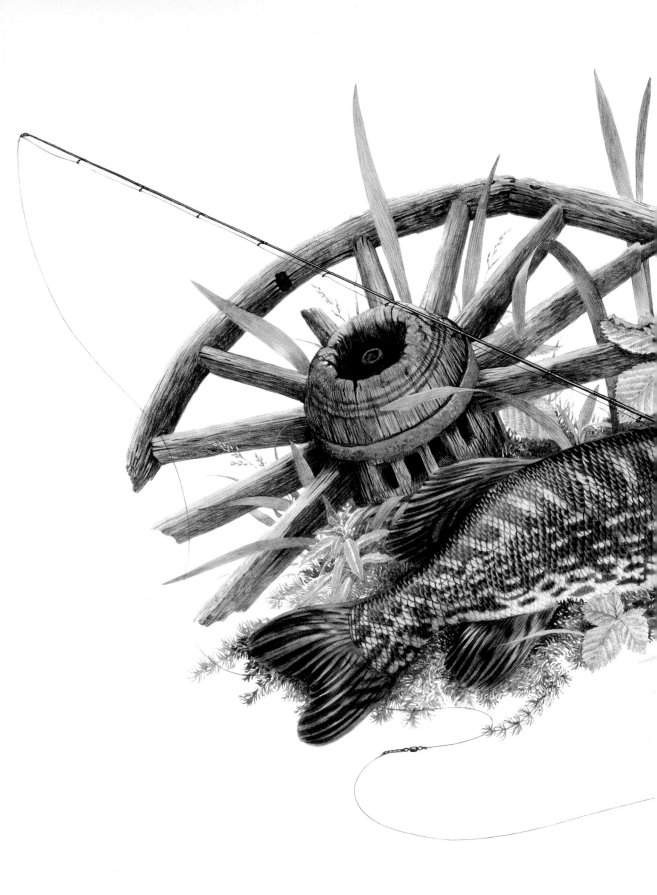

WHILE MY FLOAT'S STILL COCKED

M.J.PLEDGER

WHILE MY FLOAT'S STILL COCKED

The ramblings of an artist-angler

MAURICE J PLEDGER

Coch-y-Bonddu Books
2011

WHILE MY FLOAT'S STILL COCKED

Written and illustrated by Maurice J Pledger

First published by Coch-y-Bonddu Books Ltd, Machynlleth, 2011

Standard Edition
High-quality paperback with flaps
ISBN 978 1 904784 31 9

Collector's Edition
Limited to 250 signed cloth-bound copies
ISBN 978 1 904784 30 2

De luxe leather-bound edition of only 55 copies
Hand-bound in Nigerian goatskin by Ludlow Bookbinders
each containing a mounted float, hand-made by Paul Cook
ISBN 978 1 904784 33 3

These editions © Coch-y-Bonddu Books Ltd, Machynlleth, 2011
Text and Illustrations © Maurice J Pledger
courtesy of Bernard Thornton Artists, London
Introduction © Chris Yates 2011

Coch-y-Bonddu Books Ltd, Machynlleth, Powys SY20 8DG
01654 702837
www.anglebooks.com

FOR MY MUM & DAD

From these beginnings...

...how can I have helped but continue...

...to follow the stream

Acknowledgements

For many years I've been prompted by friends and other poor unknowing souls, to 'write a fishing book'. Not least of these are Anthony Johnson and his two brothers Matt and Lewis, the owners of Johnson Ross in Hoddesdon, my local fishing tackle shop.

From the moment I started it became a natural flow, meandering through memories that have lived with me and enriched my life beyond mere words. So many people to thank, and for so many reasons, but to list them all here would pre-empt my story. As you come to meet them along the way you will begin to understand why I thank them so much for everything. One day, hopefully far far away when I can unfortunately no longer fish, it is these memories that will keep me going, keep me smiling and live with me until my float finally dips away.

To my family and friends; you'll never know how much I appreciate and treasure your love and friendship. My wife Pietra, and my children Douglas and Laura, who have always been with me along the way. Mum and Dad, although Dad is sadly no longer with us; Dad, you would have loved this. And big brother Doug – who lit the candle.

For this page of thanks and acknowledgement my heart needs to mention a few people without whose support and belief this book would have remained no more than a passing thought.

Chris Yates; I smile every time I think of you, and am truly honoured that you have written these very kind words. I only hope that it didn't hold you up too long from your tea-brewing; that would have been unforgivable. Shooting stars need to have someone to watch over them. I'm afraid you're it.

Bernard Thornton, my agent and dear friend, you'll know what this all means. Thank you.

Paul Curtis who, unbelievably, read it all through and within not too long handed it back to me as if it had never been touched. Touched it had been, and by a magic hand.

Pete MacKenzie for being blessed with an artistic eye for how things should be, and designing and arranging everything exactly as I would have done myself.

Paul Morgan of Coch-y-Bonddu Books; what can I say? Thank you for having the vision and belief in what I have done.

Hopefully there will be enough Pixie Dust in these pages to please anyone who decides to spend time in our company. I hope that this book brings you all nothing but good things.

M3.PLEDGER

INTRODUCTION

Thirty years ago I received an invitation to a private view of an exhibition of paintings by Maurice Pledger, an artist whose work I was not familiar with. The exhibition was in a small provincial gallery near Guildford and though I really liked the reproduction Maurice had used to illustrate the invitation I really had no idea what to expect when I walked through the door. To say I was impressed would be an understatement – covering the gallery walls was a wonderful collection of bird paintings, together with a couple of stunning fish portraits. They were all painted with such finesse and with such attention to detail that the birds almost flew out of their frames while the fish almost flipped into the air.

It was great to meet the artist, too, a very modest, unassuming man who was more keen to talk about fishing than he was to discuss his work. Though he was committed to his art, fishing, he said, was his passion.

A few years later I got an invite to another of Maurice's exhibitions, this time at a more prestigious gallery in London. While the paintings were as technically brilliant as before there was a greater freedom of expression, more character in the subjects and, best of all, more fish! Since then, Maurice has gone on to become one of the finest fish and bird painters in the country whose work has been sought by collectors and regularly published in journals and fine art books.

But all the time he was working he was always planning his next escape to a favourite river or lake and it's good to discover in these pages exactly where he escaped to and what occurred when he eventually cast out. The stories from Maurice's boyhood fizz with enthusiasm and there's no doubt that his early experiences and observations were the inspiration for his artistic life. However, what marks this book out as something special is the remarkable series of fish paintings, fish with so much natural beauty and grace that they almost swim off the page.

Chris Yates
Tollard Royal, Wiltshire 2011

First Words

If you'd asked me, when I was nine years old, to finish off the sentence 'Forty-three years ago…' then in all honesty and given the off-the-wall way in which my mind was already forming, I'd probably have replied 'dinosaurs ruled the earth,' and quietly looking over my shoulder would have half believed it.

Forty-three years on, I'm looking back to the same little boy of nine, his chest heaving with excitement, eyes wide as two half crowns, as he watched his big brother Doug (then twenty-two) carefully place three eight-inch crucian carp into a neighbour's pond after we'd returned from an evening's fishing at our local Barclay Park lake in Hoddesdon. I hadn't caught them, of course – Doug had. Closing my eyes, I can see them now in the torchlight, those fish, gently spilling from his canvas water bucket through the lilies and into the little pond in the headmaster's back garden.

We lived a mere five minutes' walk away from the park. Doug used to take me there to fish for the crucians. I would use use his five-foot solid glass spinning rod and a big wide heavy wooden centrepin reel which clicked as loud as lollysticks in bike wheels. Other memories: a lovely big red-tipped cork float, line miles too thick, and a bronze eyed hook about size 10 which had been lovingly picked from a jumble of about twenty million in one of Dad's Old Holborn tobacco tins. Doug made me some bread paste, which I rolled up into balls as tight as bullets and used as bait, and of course this is why I caught nothing. I can see my float and bait now in two feet of water with a shoal of small crucians and roach swimming round it like Red Indians circling cowboys in a desert. Not one of those fish came within three feet of any of it. I treasure that memory now but I wouldn't have given you two conkers for it forty-three years ago.

And so this is my book. I won't explain what it is to be because as with all good things the enjoyment lies in finding out for yourself. I hope though that it might be a little different to any fishing book you've ever read before. You'll meet my friends, of course. You'll be hearing about Vince and Scotty, who, against their better judgement, have put up with me since we met in grammar school when we were eleven; you'll hear about Chad too, who really should have known better. I suppose they may have looked on me as you would a great snarled bird's nest around your reel. There'd be no mileage at all in trying to get rid of it, since you'd be there forever: you must simply fish on and hope for the best.

As we progress and as the mood takes, you may find other dear friends popping in to say 'Hello'. There'll be no rhyme or reason to any of this, so treat it as you would a few days' fishing in places you've never been to before. Pick up your favourite rod, shoulder your creel and we'll amble along the grassy bank, away to where a mist is forming…

Vince's Record Perch

Walking through the mist the familiar springiness of the long grass underfoot gives way after a few seconds to the feel of walking along a tow-path. As the whiteness of the swirling mist burns off I can see the distinct forms of two familiar figures fishing either side of a big bank of reeds just below Aqueduct Lock on the River Lea in Turnford. They look, these figures, as if they're around fourteen years old. Unmistakably, the one nearer the lock on the upstream edge of the reeds is Vince. The other is me.

It's a long long time ago, the start of the new season, 1969. We'd caught the first bus of the morning before dawn, and had walked forever to reach these swims. I think the reason we stopped where we did was because I was through my boots and had walked so far that my legs had worn down to the knees. I foolishly struggled for an hour with a three-hook paternoster which I was convinced would catch me three times as many bleak, three times as quickly. Vince was fishing for tench and had lost three fish in quick succession, float fishing lob worms just out from the reeds. Meanwhile, I was just in a mess. Take my word for it, if you ever have an hour to spare at least use it float fishing lob worms. Don't bother doing what I did. It isn't – it wasn't – worth it.

Vince's swim went off the boil and he started to get the fidgets. I'd already wandered off to a small pit lying just behind us, which I suppose at one time was attached to the very last bay of the North Met Pit. It was now a separate small water, but covered in old planks, plastic bottles and other rubbish. At the end nearest to us was a clearish spot, which I cast into. My little porcupine quill cocked, dipped, went under – and up came a little silver bream. A couple more followed so I quickly hopped back to Vince, collected all my gear and him along with it, and we set up in our luxurious new surroundings.

Float fishing maggots a couple of rod lengths out, we immediately began to catch small perch and silver bream – nothing over six inches, but great fun. For some reason, and I still can't explain why, I just wanted to watch a nice big red float, so off came the tiny porcupine quill and on went a red-tipped cork affair, one of Doug's 'crucian frighteners' from way back. On went a big lobworm and I dropped the lot in the water about a foot from my rod rest. It wasn't long before this paragon of a float started bobbing and dithering to such an extent that I began questioning the logic of putting something on that would have probably held up a couple of diving mallards. At some point I must have struck, because my rod hooped over and I found myself playing something that was actually swimming the other way.

To a fourteen-year-old boy accustomed to six-inch perch, bleak, gudgeon and the like, a one-pound tench was like nothing on earth. It was a foot long, for God's sake. It was huge; it had massive fins; it was bronze and gold and green and it hid half the landing net. Boy, was this a fish. It went into my keepnet with the silver bream, all the perch having already been placed in Vince's net because he didn't want his own keepnet slimed.

A subsequent half hour of nothing saw me changing back to my little porcupine, and joining Vince, who was catching a few more small perch on maggots. The fact that Vince filched my last worm initiated a sequence of events that remains my most vivid fishing memory. The subsequent hoop in Vince's rod left neither of us in any doubt that my last lobworm had attached itself to something very serious indeed. For several minutes the fish stayed deep; it wasn't until we saw the float slowly coming up that we began to think Vince might actually land whatever was on the other end. Being on quite a high bank, we had a good aerial view down onto and through the water, and because of the tench I'd just caught, I suppose we were both convinced it might be another one.

Up came the float, followed by the most stupendously huge perch either of us had ever seen. I can remember saying,

'It's a record, it's a record…'

I netted it, feverishly repeating the words

'It's a record…'

Trembling, shaking… I didn't know what to do. God knows how Vince was faring. We weighed this beast of a fish (the then record was just over four pounds), and couldn't believe the scales lied to us: 2lb 4oz those scales read – when every other indicator in our minds, eyes, heads and hearts said it should have weighed in excess of the record. For two young lads used to feasting on a diet of six-inch perch, one this size would surely have turned every set of scales in the tackle shop into clock springs.

To this day, should anyone ask me which one fish has affected me more than any other, then surely it must be Vince's 'record' perch. The perch he caught on my last worm.

If we slip back into the mist and amble round for a while then my mind travels even further back – back beyond Vince's perch, even Doug's crucians, to the time when I lost a very big fish indeed. I wouldn't be surprised if it was the loss of this one fish which really kept this passion for fishing burning so brightly all these years.

At the bottom of our garden was an area of trees and grassland with a couple of old air raid shelters. This led down to a little brook which is still there today. Since it was so close to our garden, Mum and Dad allowed me to play in this area, down by the brook with my friends.

The brook was mostly about six feet wide and nowhere deeper than about six inches; you could step over most of it, and jump over rocks and stones all along its length. Overhung by trees and bushes, two or three old footbridges and all manner of jungly undergrowth, it was a wonderful place to play pirates or cowboys-and-Indians… until we noticed the fish.

In isolated pockets we could see minnows and sticklebacks zipping about in panic whenever we went near. The brook also teemed with thousands of freshwater shrimps. Mum and Dad bought us little minnow-nets and our days were filled trying to catch the tiny fish. The shrimps were easy – every day we soon had enough to keep us happy, jam jars full of little creatures flicking up and down, round-and-round, like miniature horses on a carousel.

One day we began to notice larger fish. I don't know if they were always there or whether they'd been washed down from somewhere else, but in a couple of places there were pockets of what I guess now must have been dace. One spot in particular held two such fish, both about three-and-a-half inches long. This area, which the dace couldn't leave, was around twenty feet long – plenty long enough for them to remain hidden or evade capture and generally drive us insane with the desire to catch one. I remember that for days my friend Pete and I would go and try to catch these fish in our nets, and every time our efforts ended in failure. Sometimes, if the brook coloured up, we'd have to wait patiently for days for it to clear so we could stalk those two fish.

Whenever we saw the fish we tried new ways to creep up on them; our plans having been hatched up in bed the night before. If Pete wasn't possessed by the thought of these two wonderful creatures, then I certainly was.

One day, a day no different to any other, I saw one of the dace idly hanging about an inch off bottom, just under the other bank and about a foot from it. My tactics had evolved to the extent that I now preferred to get into the brook, coming up on those fish from behind. There was no flow. I crept ever nearer and gently closed in with the net. Even by the age of nine, I'd taught myself through observation how to keep my eyes firmly fixed on the fish, and whatever movement I'd make would depend on its movements and reactions. If it showed any change whatsoever in its manner – an agitation of a fin or a slight alertness in its eyes – I'd stop. After the fish had relaxed, I'd continue. After a longish while, I'd got the net to within an inch of its tail without the dace knowing I was there.

I knew I couldn't slowly glide the fish into the net. The only option was a quick upwards lift. I can still see the moment now, a point of frozen time spanning the split second in which I made my final play. As the net swept up and broke the surface of the water, the fish was balanced perfectly on the rim – half-in, half-out. And as the cascade of spray fell back to the brook, so too did the fish.

In the days that followed I still kept trying but I never did catch either of those two fish. That one sublime moment was the nearest I ever came.

It was about this time that brother Doug, seeing that I'd developed an interest in fishing, started to take me to Barclay Park.

M.J.PLEDGER

HANGING UP MY MINNOW NET

The transition from minnow net to fishing rod was a natural one. I'd been used to seeing Doug's fishing tackle in the shed, and on occasion must have secretly sneaked in and gone through his rod-bags. The rod that I really gravitated towards was a five-foot, solid glass spinning-rod, dark in colour, and to my eyes, magical. I liked to go through his floats, arranging and rearranging them. I used to count his split shot, sort out all the bits and pieces and put them all back again, usually in a better state than when he'd left them, just like I did with my whole collection of fireworks around bonfire night – all the Catherine wheels, airplanes and jumping crackers. There was something quite comforting about a busy tackle box with lots in it. I felt like Gulliver, custodian of the treasure of Lilliput, making sure everything was in its place.

Then one day either Doug, or Mum and Dad, bought me a lovely five-foot white solid glass spinning rod. When Doug took me to the park I used the big wooden centrepin with my new rod, but it was while we were on our next holiday in Mum's hometown of Bologna in Italy that Dad bought me my first reel. It was the best reel in the shop, a Mitchell 314. That reel must have been the most loved, most handled and most polished reel in history. How on earth I didn't wear out every gear in it even before it got anywhere near any water must rank alongside the world's greatest unexplained mysteries.

Of course, by this time I'd helter-skeltered into fishing, which as a passion now rivalled drawing and bird watching. Therefore it was inevitable that pocket money from Mum, Dad, Doug, Nanny Queenie and Granddad Alf would now find a new destination: Ross's, the tackle shop in Hoddesdon.

Bit by bit my little tackle box filled. The days were a wonderful, heady mix of drawing, bird watching, fishing with Doug… and hay fever.

I remember Doug showing me how to gently unhook the first few crucians I ever caught, fish of perhaps no more than four or five inches long, and I suppose it must have been at this point that I truly considered myself a fisherman.

For the last year of primary school I also fished with Pete, who lived up the road. Our usual haunt was the park but we also tried the gravel pit near Admiral's Walk, another five minutes' walk away. I used to go bird watching around there with Dad and had got to know the place really well, so I think Mum and Dad realised it was okay for me to fish there if I was with Pete. Here we fished for pike with a pound-and-a-half of sprats bought from Brewster's, the fishmonger in town, and with pike traces and bungs from Ross's next door. We caught one or two small pike on most trips.

Moving on to Broxbourne Grammar School, as it was then, at the age of eleven, making new friends in my class was entirely dependent on who went fishing. I'd already known Chad all the way through primary school and although we were really good friends we hadn't yet fished together. Then a beam of light must have shone in from somewhere and somehow dragged this new kid over to us.

'Hello, I'm Vince.'

Vince was the catalyst. From that day on, the three of us were inseparable both in the classroom and on the riverbank. Although there was an outer circle of fishing friends in our classroom, we three always stayed together. In fact, the very first time Vince and I went fishing together it was in a larger gathering at the gravel pit at Admiral's Walk. We were all piking, and not having too much luck. I'd been sitting in one spot for about five hours with a sprat dying a thousand deaths of loneliness in a misbegotten swim which belied its attractiveness. Amazed at my own patience, I finally gave in to sense, reeled in and moved further along the bank. Vince moved into my just vacated spot, cast out and promptly caught a pike of 9lb, which bettered my heaviest pike by 3lb 8oz.

From that day to this, I've pulled this little trick on Vince so many times that it's ceased to surprise him. In fact I think he almost expects it.

The transition to fisherman was complete.

THE SIXPENCE JAR

On rare occasions throughout my life everything seems to come together to form the perfect moment. I'm sure we've all felt such moments. For me, these moments are so perfect that there have been times I've leant back in my fishing chair, placed my hands behind my head, breathed in deeply and quietly said to myself, 'I just wish this moment would never end.' I suppose it's happened most often, but not exclusively, when I've been fishing. I think because fishing brings together so many of life's wonders that it's easy for the perfect moment to form. We just have to be conscious of it happening and appreciate it when it does. Such a moment can translate into the most enduring of memories.

Whenever I wish on a special moment, it's like dropping an old silver sixpence into a big jar. Once the coin has tinkled in with the rest, the moment will never end; it will always be there for me whenever I need it again.

One of the best such moments didn't actually happen while I was fishing, but thanks to the sixpence jar, it is still as fresh today as it was forty-six years ago. My mum and I were with Auntie Laura and Uncle Sergio in Bologna in Northern Italy, being driven out in the car one evening to some low-lying hills where we were told we would see *stelle cadente* – falling stars. For the next twenty minutes, my face was pressed against the window as I looked in the passing fields hoping to see great, glowing, implausibly star-shaped stars half-buried in the ground where they'd crash-landed. I was out of my skin in wonder and wished the night would never end. When the car pulled up and we all got out and everyone looked skywards, of course I began to see the shooting stars the adults had been talking about. The only let-down was that I couldn't go and run over to one of these falling stars, touch it, clamber all over it and maybe slide down the sides.

Nonetheless, the first sixpence had surely been dropped in the jar of memory and these delicious moments are there for me whenever I need them.

The sixpence jar was working overtime a few years ago at the lovely Blickling Lake in Norfolk. Scotty and I arrived before daybreak with our good friends Dave and Steve. In all our years of fishing I've never been witness to a more glorious birth of a fishing day than that one. The dark watercolours of night struggled to wash into the warm ambers and oranges of a rising sun but were held back by a damp mist which seemed to hang on forever. Silent forms wandered in the field behind us, adding to the dream. Disconcerted, I asked more learned minds than mine about these unearthly shapes and was told that these forms were searching for magic mushrooms.

Flocks of Egyptian geese took to the air. Momentarily silhouettes, they rose out of the mist, catching the first rays of sunlight; rose through another bank of mist; then were gone. Sitting in our own separate swims, we each of us had our own story to tell. Scott and I confirmed after a couple of hours that although this indeed was the perfect dawn, the fish were cagey beyond belief, both of us experiencing only the most minute bite indications and twitches of our lines.

At Dave's swim, Steve was sitting behind Dave's rod, leaning back in a garden chair reading a newspaper, while Dave was trying to tidy up after the manic episode of a missed bite. This bite had taken his indicator all the way into the butt, sent the Optonic howling and his swingtip straight, before his rod fell off the rests and was nearly dragged in. But then, after all, this is Dave.

Along this same bank, but on a different day, I think Scott and I each dropped a sixpence in the jar for Dave. A moment that surely warranted a shilling's worth of anyone's money.

Scott and I were both tucked under our umbrellas in the reeds, sheltering as best we could from the deluge of rain which was falling on Blickling that late afternoon. Only twice in my life have I witnessed rain to match it. Visibility was down to perhaps no more than two swims, and I imagined thronged masses in New Delhi were at that moment giving praise that this particular monsoon had passed them by. At the extreme limit of our vision we could see a figure standing bolt upright at the end of one of the fishing stages, head angled slightly down, looking at the lake. If I had to describe the expression on his face, I don't think 'forlorn' would have been far wrong.

Wondering just what the hell was going on, we watched as the figure remained standing there. After an age it became obvious that it was Dave. When, a little later, we quietly edged round for an explanation, he was quite matter-of-fact about the whole thing, saying that he'd just got soaked through changing swims – so wet, in fact, that because he couldn't possibly get any wetter, he thought he might as well stand out in it.

A NOSE FOR THE RIDICULOUS

Tucked away among the good memories are the not so good. Let's face it, even bad memories, when we're safely well away from them, can be remembered in a more favourable light than on the days we suffered them. I also realise that a great many of the memories that really stand out don't actually involve fish at all.

Still, this one did.

One day a few years ago I was having a field day with the chub at one of my favourite haunts, King's Weir on the River Lea. I was probably on my third chub when I looked over to Dave in the barbel swim. Dave was staring dolefully at his rod tip, which was looking back at him in an even less interested way. I called over to him to come and join me in catching a few chub. Given his lack of luck with any kind of fish at the time, or any time come to that, his deadpan reply came drifting back:

'I'd sooner be not catching barbel than not catching chub.'

And while we're in the realm of wisdom which is Dave…

He once told me how years ago, when he was very young, his dad would try to teach him how to be quiet by the waterside by sitting him beside a washing-up bowl full of water in his back garden. I always thought it a shame there isn't a photo. Unless Dave's keeping it from me.

One memory I'd dearly like to shake off, but can't, is the phone call.

I was fourteen. I was due to meet Scotty somewhere down by the Crown on the Lea at three in the morning. As usual, I couldn't sleep, and during the night it had begun to rain the rain of the damned. By 2 a.m. I could only just open the back door against winds that would have had Arctic terns heading back home. For some reason I thought Scotty would be awake as well, so I just picked up the phone and dialled the number. Of course, everyone in his house was fast asleep, and Scott's dad, unfortunately, kept the phone right by his bed. I heard him answer, in a Scotty's-dad-fast-asleep kind of way, and thrown by this, I could only find two words in my head:

'It's raining.'

I've often wondered if I could have phrased it better or somehow emphasise on the fact that if the rain continued then by about 3 a.m. the chub would be coming through the letterbox.

When I was eleven and was deemed old enough to be allowed to use maggots by the powers that oversaw such matters, I felt I'd grown up. By the time I'd bought my third pint of the creatures, I was troubled. I'd begun to wonder if maggots ever slept, so one evening I crept out to the shed several times and, carefully lifting the lid off the bait box, shone a torch inside. Did they ever sleep? They never did.

Nineteen-sixty-nine must have been a good year for cultivating silly memories, or perhaps my stars were in perfect alignment with Scotty's, allowing stupid things to happen. On one particular afternoon, we were piking on a local gravel pit near Admiral's Walk in Hoddesdon. I think we may have even caught two or three jacks on free-lined sprats, so things were looking good. Wandering off, I'd found a dead great crested grebe floating near the edge of the bank, and seeing that you don't come across one of these that often, I took it back to show Scott. Drifting, half-submerged among the flotsam of the shore didn't seem a fitting end for a bird of such nobility, so we decided to give it a decent Viking send-off.

I found a small wooden board which would serve as a long boat, propped up the grebe's head with a forked stick in a suitably proud posture, and just to finish things off, Scotty lit a cigarette and shoved it in the bird's beak. After a couple of false starts, the funeral boat finally began to drift and the last we saw of it, it was proudly heading out into the gravel pit while the bird had its proverbial last cigarette.

Another time when I was fishing with Steve I saw this big black lump in the middle of a freshly ploughed field some ninety yards away. It bothered me, not knowing what this big black lump was. And it kept bothering me to such an extent that I really had to go and find out what it was. It wasn't that it was in my line of vision while I was looking out across the gravel pit, because from where I was sitting I couldn't see it even if I wanted to. I had to get off my chair, climb up a vertical almost cliff-like gravel bank of fifteen feet, face completely in the other direction, look into a howling east wind and squint through watery eyes to see it.

But there it was: the black lump.

After three hours of this torment I left Steve sitting there below the cliff watching the rods, while I trudged off over the ploughed field to solve the mystery. During the trudge my mind went through every possible permutation of what this 'thing' could be. A discarded bag of cash from a bank robbery? Treasure unearthed by the plough? Aladdin's lamp? My mind was wandering. Yes, a big bag of cash – it couldn't possibly be anything else.

By the time I'd made the last ten yards, trying to walk into a dire east wind with muddied feet that now felt like lead diving boots, I was completely out of breath and, seemingly, out of luck. There before me lay the biggest turnip I'd ever seen. Nevertheless, I picked it up and made my way back. Approaching the top of the cliff with my prize, I couldn't see Steve anywhere. The only thing I could do in the circumstances was reel in his line and tie the thing onto his hook. This took some doing: the turnip was about the size of a small football and as heavy as a bucket of wet sand. I opened the bail arm, carefully placed Steve's rod on the rests, and walked back to the top of the cliff above the swim, whereupon I heaved the turnip out as far as I could.

Thinking something this heavy would doubtless sink like a lump of flint, I was totally surprised that seconds after the cataclysmic splash, the stupid thing came bobbing back up. I went back down, sat in my chair and waited for Steve. On his return I pointed out the strange black lump floating out in the gravel pit. Now it was his turn to sit there, wondering what it was… until his indicator started crawling up…

Then there was the night when Scott, Dave, Steve and I were in Dave's mum's caravan in the Sheringham caravan park. We were all in our sleeping bags, had switched off the lights and said goodnight. It was now dark and perfectly quiet – for about one minute. Quite why Steve's mention of the bailiff's nose set me off on such a fit of giggles I'll never know – nor how we lived through the next twenty minutes without choking to death.

We'd spent the day fishing a lovely lake near Sheringham. I'd better not mention its name in case the bailiff in question reads this. As in the past, just after first light we could see his distant form along the bank approaching through the morning mist. He was a fine, gentle old sort: quiet, friendly, Norfolk accent, an old furry suit jacket, baggy trousers and Wellington boots; eyes quite close set, warm face – but with this great big red nose. A really great big red nose. A really, really, great big red nose.

I politely asked what time we were allowed to start fishing, to which he replied, 'Six.' Now, my mouth habitually runs off some utter rubbish before my brain kicks in, and I replied, questioningly, 'Sex?' At this point the bailiff, usually a friendly, talkative type, clammed up completely, backed off up the bank and hurried off into the mist from whence he'd come.

Which accounts I suppose for the hilarity over Steve saying the word 'nose'. And also why, for the rest of the trip, I had to suffer ridiculous accusations of having made sexual advances to Norfolk bailiffs.

JUNK TACKLE JUNKIE

Someone once said that the single most important item of fishing tackle was the hook. He was right. The amount of tackle some anglers think they need to help them dangle a length of line and a hook in the water really must border on the excessive. I decided to prove the point. For a little while I became obsessed with finding the most basic, cheapest, fishing tackle I could, then going out and catching a really good fish on it – thereby proving that the all-important part of the tackle is what is on the hook, and not at the other end. This minimalism was my new quest.

When I was ten, the rod I really wanted was a tiny little two-piece, wiry-looking thing you could buy in Woolworth's. I remember it being about four feet long and coming attached to a piece of cardboard which inevitably had some kind of wizard advertising on it. However or whatever it was marketed, labelled or sold as, that rod must have rated as being up there with the pyramids in my book. If Woolworth's sold more than one of these rods to a real fisherman though, then the advertising director should surely have been rewarded with the Keys of England.

Later I tried everywhere but sadly couldn't find anything like that Woolworth's rod. For days I looked round every conceivable kind of toyshop, and was shown several times (and by several nice ladies) various plastic specials from Care Bears to Smurfs. Perhaps I hadn't explained myself clearly enough. I finally got lucky in my local tackle shop. Out came a Japanese children's outfit costing £7.95. The rod looked a suitable bright silver and had four bent wire rings and a lovely cheap plastic handle. I ditched the reel because it was too good; I'd got something else in mind. I would have bought the girl's version of the rod, in bright fluorescent pink, but sadly they didn't have one in stock. I was pleased to find I could bend the rod into almost a complete circle without the slightest effort. If I had to find one word which would have best described all its attributes, I think 'dire' would have been entirely appropriate. The reel I had on order from somewhere else, and a few days later it finally arrived; green and white and made of metal, about two-and-a-half inches across, this was The Winfield Centrepin, a Woolworth's special from the misty days a million years ago when they sold their own brand of fishing tackle. This reel wouldn't spin even if you got a donkey to kick it. You could hear that centrepin's click down the street. It was perfect. I put on some 8lb line and I was ready.

My river of choice was a little stretch of the Lea at Hertingfordbury one mild rainy night in late autumn. The swim was a favourite of mine – only twenty feet wide, just below a sharp bend. It was shallow at my feet, with a six-foot deep gully running along the opposite bank under a canopy of overhanging branches. Over the years we'd found that the barbel cruised up this gully after dark. Any bait placed in their path was likely to be taken without too much hesitation.

Because I couldn't cast as normal with this Reel of Satan, I had to pull off the amount of line I thought I'd need and let it fall at my feet, then swing the lot out. Carefully judging everything and trusting entirely to luck, I managed to put the first cast exactly where I wanted. My end-tackle was a short fixed paternoster with a longish trail, a size 4 hook and a big cube of luncheon meat.

It was now dark. The rain was gentle and warm and the current was running nicely coloured, pushing through about eighteen inches higher than usual. With all these positives in my favour, it came as no surprise that I had only to wait about twenty seconds for my first bite, a nice, solid thump which I missed completely, as I did the next... and the next... and the next... Finally sorting out the mechanics of striking with a rod just twice the length of my arm, my fifth strike met with solid resistance. My poor little rod took on five kinds of bends and threatened to continue the same up my forearm. Clamping down on the tiny reel, I could hear it mechanically hacking and clacking, not knowing whether to give line or whether the reel would allow me to retrieve it – or just explode. The barbel heaved a wave through the confines of the swim like a dolphin in a paddling pool. I had to scramble to my feet in the mud and try and subdue what was obviously a very large fish on my Lilliputian rod and reel. Everything performed exactly as I expected, and after a manic five minutes I glided a very surprised barbel over the landing net. If there had been a shoal moving through, then the fifth bite was a good one to hook because the fish turned out to be my very best barbel: 9lb 11oz. Ten minutes later it seemed there was a little more magic left in the evening when another barbel of 7lb came to pay a visit.

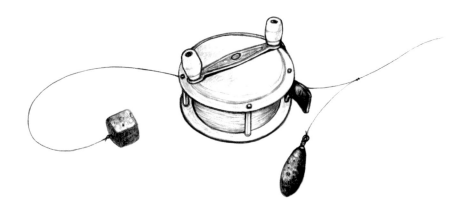

PELICANS AND STONEFISH, USA

It was summer 1991 when my wife Pietra, son Douglas, daughter Laura, and I took a family holiday to Walt Disney World in Florida. We spent our second week at St. Petersburg, recovering from the first. When I discovered that our hotel was only a short three minute drive from the sea, it was simplicity itself for to sniff out the local tackle shop and equip myself with a cheap spinning rod and reel and enough bits and pieces to enable me to cast out a line. Since the rest of the family had no real interest in fishing, I decided the only way I could grab myself a couple of hours was to go while everyone was still asleep, early in the morning. As we tended to get up around 8 a.m., I set my alarm for five thirty and managed to sneak out while it was still dark without too much trouble. I'd then return at eight to find them just waking up, so the only person who was missing out on anything was me. I'd simply be deprived of sleep – which, when fishing was concerned, wasn't a consideration.

Arriving in the dark, I pulled up along the edge of the sea front on a road bordering a wide, sweeping bay. Along this bay, at intervals of about fifty yards, were long fishing jetties reaching out into the water which, I suppose, at the extremities of the jetties twenty yards out, was about ten feet deep. I chose one of these jetties at random, walked out to the end, sat with legs dangling over the edge and tackled up. I tied up a simple fixed paternoster with a sixteen-inch hook link and light ¼oz Arlesey bomb, size 6 hook and 5lb line. For bait I cut up small cubes of luncheon meat from a standard large can. I flicked out the bait on my first cast, and idly sat there with the line crooked over my finger waiting for… anything. As darkness gave way to a watery dawn I began to make out shark-like fins cutting through the calm waters further out into the bay. Feeling slightly uneasy about dangling my legs only a few feet over the water's surface, I brought them back fully over the edge of the jetty, felt a sharp tug on the line and hooked into something which hooped the little rod. For a good five minutes I played the unseen fish and eventually lifted out a catfish of over two pounds.

It was a very welcome first result, but the fins cutting back and forth unsettled me, so I moved back nearer the car and fished off the wall. It was only after a further half an hour, when things got light enough to see clearly through my binoculars, that I saw the fins actually belonged to dolphins, so I moved back out to the end of the jetty. Then I began to get a bite a cast, tugs being felt immediately the bait hit bottom, the culprits being silvery, bream-like fish of between six ounces and half a pound. After I'd returned the sixth or seventh of these lovely fish, I heard a great flapping of wings behind my back and a skidding thump. Wondering just what the hell had nearly used me as a landing strip, I turned my head and looked straight into the beady eyes of a massive brown pelican, head angled upwards, eyes reminiscent of Jack Elam on a bad day, wings outstretched and beak wide open.

Having just been cut off from the outside world by this relic of the Jurassic, I began to strike up a conversation with him, and it didn't take me one second to realise he wanted feeding. I cast out and hooked another of the silver bream. When the pelican saw the rod take on a curve, he got very agitated and started hopping around and snapping his beak. I lifted out the fish, unhooked it and tossed it in his general direction. I don't think he even tasted it. This ridiculous state of affairs went on for the next hour, during which we were joined by several of his mates, a grey heron and two white egrets. I was mobbed by an audience of birds. Whenever I struck and missed a bite they all calmed down, and whenever the rod curved they all began to leap about, wings flapping, and wouldn't stop until I threw the fish among them. A great snapping of leaping beaks ensued about three feet from my face. The odd thing was that they all realised when a fish threw the hook, because when the rod was curved over and a fish was being played they'd all go into a manic dance. If the rod tip sprang back straight, they would all, immediately and as one, stop and sit quite still until the next one was being played – when they'd whoop it up again.

It was then I struck into a small catfish of about ten inches. The bird audience began to immediately cower and back off down the jetty, some of them flapping and falling off the edge, until only one pelican and the grey heron remained. Out of interest I held the catfish and offered it to them, but in the end I let it go, as it obviously scared them to death. The only thing that I could think of that would provoke such a reaction was the long spine on the leading edge of the catfish's dorsal fin. Whether they'd all learned the hard way, or whether the lesson had been handed down by their parents, I'd never know. In any event, catfish, it seemed, were safe. Once I'd thrown the culprit back, they all hopped back on board the jetty and resumed partying with the bream.

Until this point I'd been flicking the bait out a few yards, so by way of a change I lowered the next one down by one of the platform supports, which had around it, as did the other supports, a pile of sub-surface rocks. A sharp tug followed, with the rod really crawling over into a heavy fish and the line instantly snapping. Taken by surprise, I re-tackled, dropped the bait down and once again, experienced ten seconds of struggling with something which really didn't want to come up, then the line parting as before. Checking the line for the second time, I found that the last couple of feet were really sandpapered, suggesting that the fish could have been a large eel of some kind – maybe poking its head out of the rocks to pick up the bait, then dragging itself back into its lair, leaving me with no chance of playing it out. I knew it was pointless to try again, so I packed up, said goodbye to my overfed avian companions, and went back to the hotel room just in time for the alarm clock.

I told Douglas and Laura about the morning's events, and Douglas was eager to return the following morning and help me out with the plan I'd devised to catch whatever it was that was sitting underneath me on the jetty. Back at the tackle shop, we bought a spool of 25lb line, a couple of thick wire traces and a few massive hooks.

Next morning we arrived in the dark as before and set up the rod with the usual gear. Douglas, however, decided he'd be left in charge of The Beastie below decks. We attached a whole can of luncheon meat to the hook (that is, a can of luncheon meat minus the can) and lowered it down the edge of the support, among the rocks. Douglas then sat back with the line over his finger. My instructions had been to give it a good yank if he felt a tug. Within minutes he sprang to his feet and I could see the line cutting this way and that, with Douggy hanging on grimly up top. Between the pair of us we managed to keep it away from the rocks, and lifted it out: a very irate stonefish of about three pounds, most of which was head. Since stonefish are poisonous in the extreme, we let it dangle just below the edge of the woodwork while we took some photos. Then, on removing the hook with a long pair of forceps, we noticed the two lines he'd snapped the previous day, still in the side of his mouth. On being released he fell back with a loud splash and swam back down to his pile of rocks. When I related the story to the tackle shop owner, he informed us that a stonefish of that size was exceptional for the area; almost unheard of. It pleased me that 'our' stonefish had gone back to grow into an even bigger one.

THE GREAVES & THOMAS
ANGLING SOCIETY

In 1969, a year which glows in my memory, Vince and I were both fourteen years old. I remember those days with great affection. At this time my brother Doug worked at Schreiber, the furniture manufacturer in Hoddesdon, at Rye House on the banks of the River Lea. Anyone who worked at Schreiber was entitled to join the Greaves & Thomas Angling Society, the angling club of their sister company in Harlow, of which Doug was already a senior member. Because I was his little brother, and because Vince was my good friend, strings were pulled and we both enrolled as juniors. They were wonderful times. Monthly coach trips were arranged which went to various waters dotted around the South of England – waters which we otherwise would never have been allowed to fish. If I remember correctly, Vince and I were usually the only two juniors to show up at all the matches, so most of the attention, if any attention was given, centred on the pair of us. As always, we contrived to fish together wherever we went, so every trip turned into what was simply a great day out fishing, with the added incentive of beating the pants off each other.

For some reason, perhaps because I was Doug's little brother, there must have been some incentive for all Doug's mates in the club to treat me as some kind of whipping-boy. Given this apparently natural order of things, I resigned myself to all kinds of underhand treatment by the older members. Doug's friends often used to add colour to their day by darkening mine.

I well remember one nice sunny afternoon on the Thames. I was quite happily sitting alongside Vince, catching a few ruffe and bleak, watching a flotilla of twenty swans aimlessly cruising just off our rod tops. Doug and my cousin Chris came ambling along the bank, hands behind their backs, and began enquiring how the fishing was going. I was about halfway through replying that the fishing was going quite well when they heaved what amounted to a full loaf of chopped-up bread all over our rods – leaving us to live through the carnage only twenty hungry mute swans could cause.

I was the butt of pranks not only on club outings but also on club meetings at a pub in Harlow. On one occasion, my socks were forcibly taken off and thrown out of an upper storey, ivy-clad window. It was while I was leaning out of the window to retrieve them that I was set on by a gang of Doug's mates and dangled upside down from the sash, probably in an effort to help me get the socks back. When this didn't work, I was chased barefoot through the crowded pub into the car park and beyond, into the dead of night. On finding that Doug and his mate had driven off without me, I started the long walk home, but was eventually relieved when, after some long while, they returned to pick me up. I was shoehorned into the back of the little white van amongst a whole array of loose trays, work tools, boxes and other stuff which I couldn't see in the darkness but which flew and banged around me at every twist and turn while we hurtled at unheard of speeds around the winding country lanes towards Hoddesdon. I thought, wrongly as it turned out, that Gordon the driver would maybe hit the brake pedal at some point – and preferably, fifty yards in front of the rickety old level crossing. But Gordon continued at whatever speed his foot, which was already pushed through the floor, determined – I'm guessing seventy miles per hour. Or more.

On hitting the tracks, the van took to the sky, seemed to travel endlessly through the air and crashed back onto the road, skidding to a halt half way down the street. And this is where it stayed, because the impact, apart from almost shaking all my teeth from my head, had ripped the body of the van off the wheels. After we all got out and stood back to look at the thing among plumes of smoke, the van didn't really look too bad. It just didn't start. It never started again.

Another episode I can't forget was being left on my own to walk towards a huge black bull which was actually pawing the ground, head bowed, and was obviously in a mind to destroy whatever was in front of it. Along with Doug and a gathering of his brave fishing buddies, I was walking back across a field from a day's fishing at Godmanchester on the River Ouse. Thinking there was safety in numbers, we confidently strode towards this increasingly-irritated beast, when on looking round, I saw the rest of them had stopped, leaving me to walk the last seventy or eighty yards completely on my own. Fortunately, though, at the last moment the stupid animal decided against wearing me as an ornament, and just stood and watched as we all detoured around its field to safety.

The Wensum in Norfolk was a lovely river. Yet, for over three hours everyone who'd been on the coach wandered around in a heat wave like lost Arabs among the desert dunes as we tried in vain to find the river. A small group of us gave up and fished in a tiny lake we found, while word got through later in the day that an adventurous few had got lucky and had indeed found the river – not that it did anyone much good; the only roach caught that afternoon was unhooked by a passer-by, a helpful young lad who commented that he'd never seen a roach before. On being given permission to touch and hold the fish by the captor, who was brimming with pride that he would probably win the match with this one precious fish, the boy dropped it on the bank and it fell back in.

Another memorable outing was to Portholme Meadow on the River Ouse. A group of Hell's Angels ended up swimming in the river in front of us. This didn't improve our angling chances.

Because we were junior members, Vince and I were allowed to weigh-in bleak and gudgeon, something the seniors weren't entitled to do. On the odd occasion, one of us would catch a roach or dace, and over the period

of the season, the points between us would fluctuate, with one of us being in front of the other by just a few points, and vice versa, thereby giving the other the incentive to fish that little bit harder next trip, to win back the lead. The prize at the end of the season, to be presented at the prestigious annual dinner and dance, would in our case be the rather splendid Junior Championship Shield, with the winner's name engraved on it. This would be presented in front of the whole club with great ceremony. To an impressionable fourteen-year-old boy, this was a very big thing indeed.

We never really caught anything of note on these club outings. The club was affiliated to the London Anglers' Association, so we all had to buy an official metal LAA ruler, which had the size limits of various fish named in inches along its length: gudgeon and bleak 5″, roach and rudd 8″, bream, tench and carp 12″, dace 7″, perch 9″ and so on. Any fish caught on the day were measured on the ruler, and if they were of size, were retained in a keep-net until the end of the match. They were then transferred carefully to a canvas water bucket and taken to the weigh-in at a pre-arranged spot, usually near the fishery entrance. This was the hour of reckoning, when everyone found out who had caught what – and therefore, who had won the match and how this affected the points in the overall competition for that season's trophies.

On the return journey in the coach, for the first twenty minutes or so there would be much talk of how these latest results would affect everyone's points. These discussions were followed by boots getting kicked off, by the first snoring, and by my hat being snatched off my head yet again and being passed around the coach so that it could be filled up with all the cigarette ash and butts from the trays behind the seats – and then, of course, being politely and kindly handed back to me.

We fished various venues on the River Thames during our three seasons at Greaves & Thomas: Little Wittenham, Sonning and Sunbury Lock. No matter what the rules said or what swims we initially started in, Vince and I invariably shifted within the hour and ended up shoulder-to-shoulder fishing the same spot. On a lake this proved no problem whatsoever, but with our dexterity, we'd also manage to do it even float fishing in fast flowing water on a river too… which I suppose, if we're completely honest about things, accounts for the lack of fish caught on so many of these trips. Still, no matter, we caught some fish – and we had great times.

On the River Ouse we fished at Godmanchester (home of the massive bull), Portholme Meadow, Eaton Socon, Holmes Island and Littleport. Littleport proved a little problematic, in that when we arrived we were faced with a river miles wide, dead straight and with deeply shelving banks. Being (the Thames aside) more at home with rivers of a more intimate character, we shared one bite between us all day. This went to Vince. He foul-hooked a lamprey about an inch long and a sixteenth of an inch thick.

During the 1970-71 season I usually managed to keep just in front of Vince in the competition, if by only a few points. As we ticked off the outings towards season's end it became ever more obvious (to me at least) that the awarding of the Junior Championship Shield, marvellous big shiny thing that it was, was virtually a mere formality.

It was at this time, a momentous time in my young life, that I befriended a girl at school by the name of Julie Dust. (Befriended? It was love – true love). She and my mum and dad were invited to join me and witness what was to be my moment of triumph at the annual dinner dance when all the awards were to be presented. Before that, however, there was the last angling outing of the club season.

Grove Ferry on the Kentish Stour, March 14th, 1971, a date which even now burns a hole in my calendar of memories. The last outing, the last day of the season – fate itself couldn't have set the table more deliciously for me. The day arrived, the coach pulled up at the fishery entrance – and as usual, the river was flowing the wrong way. It always did when I'd thought about things too much, because on arrival all my plans would be thrown into turmoil: the first thing I would be faced with was the river flowing the wrong way. Then, the day was wrong. The weather was wrong.

Thankfully though, no-one had a bite. In any case I was safe because I had a margin of a few points, and luckily for me – very, very luckily for me – even if Vince and I both caught nothing, I would still be walking up in front of the whole club to collect the Junior Championship Shield. And Julie Dust would be there. Clapping in admiration along with all the others – Mum, Dad, friends, brother Doug and all his disbelieving cohorts, and of course… Vince. The vision played itself out time and time again during that miserable, biteless day.

An hour to go before the final whistle and then no more fishing for three months. The shield was mine. Already I could see it sitting on the mantelpiece instead of that stupid pot of flowers under the mirror…

'Hey, Mole, I've got a bream.'

Vince had, for once, been fishing round the corner, a couple of swims along, and it was with these words he greeted me as he came into view – beaming. Without wishing to labour the point, I think if I'd been sitting in the middle of the ocean all alone in a little boat, it would have been at that precise moment the bottom would have fallen out of it. I got up and followed him back to his swim, and it was only when I saw his keep-net fully stretched out in the water in front of him that I realised he wasn't joking. It was a formality; that I made him lift it out for me to see it, but sure enough, as sure as my bottom jaw was lying by my boots, there it was, a perfect bream, all 1lb 5oz of it.

I was never good at maths. I was never good at bream either, but I knew the two together meant that the points-difference would now be altered dramatically, but by how much I wasn't sure. It was no good returning to fish my swim so I upped all my gear and dumped it as near as I could to Vince's in the vain hope there would be another bream around just as gullible as his one. For the remaining forty-five minutes I fished my heart out – to no avail. Nothing I could do would tempt that miserable float to go under, and when the final whistle blew I was resigned to hearing some pretty unwanted news.

And so it came to pass that Vince's bream of 1lb 5oz put him in the lead overall at the very last moment. He beat me. At the dinner dance he went up to collect the magnificent shield and everyone, including Julie and myself, applauded the rotten sod.

It is now thirty-seven years later. Four or five years ago Vince happened to mention, in passing, that 'his' bream hadn't been 'completely fairly hooked in the mouth'. When I asked him to elaborate a little on this statement – it was something I'd not known about for all those intervening years – he kindly let me in on the fact that he'd actually foul-hooked it on the nose – which of course, had he mentioned it at the time, would have prevented his being allowed to weigh-in the fish.

And it would have been me who won that trophy, and maybe not lost the beautiful Julie Dust.

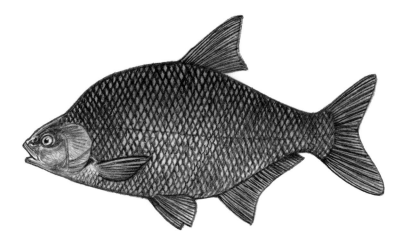

M.J.PLEDGER.

ELVIS HAS LEFT THE BUILDING

The beginning of our Norfolk fishing expedition in July 1977 started interestingly enough. Mum and Dad had already left for their holiday to Italy, and I was alone with a list of verbal instructions to lock all the windows, pull out the plugs and turn off the gas before I left the house. As I waited for Vince to come and pick me up early that Saturday morning I started on the long list of locking, pullings-out and turnings-off. Leaning on top of a large cabinet I reached down behind it and started ferreting around, trying to unplug whatever it was I imagined was down there to be unplugged. For some reason I must have shoved my fingers into something I really shouldn't have. The electric shock sent me flying across the room. And that was the start of our fishing holiday.

Vince had previously bought a car especially for the trip, an ancient Morris Oxford, and it was in this we chugged off to our destination, Rollesby in Norfolk.

On arriving at the spacious guest house, which stood in its own open, sprawling grounds, we were shown our room. This was originally an outside toilet or brick outhouse which had recently been converted into an extra room. No matter; it suited our needs admirably as it had two beds in it: a large double for Vince and a small bunk bed, which I immediately commandeered. Unfortunately, 'my' end of the room was a haven for spiders, and had to undergo a regular clear-out every time I got anywhere near the bed. Maggots, worms and groundbait were to be kept outside; a house rule which I thought was a bit off.

Anyway, we had arrived. Two weeks of pure unadulterated fishing – and it was all ours. If it were possible for two people to drop dead from pure joy, we'd have both been buried there that morning.

Unpacking took us a short five minutes. Then we went to see the owner, who pointed us in the direction of Rollesby Broad, a mere few minutes away, on which the guest house had a private rowing boat. We hastily packed whatever we thought we needed, and within half an hour we were pushing out from the reeds in the rowing boat, away from that roomful of spiders. We'd never fished from a boat before. Actually, we'd never found ourselves sitting together in a boat before, so after we'd got over the initial puzzlings about how to make the thing go forwards as opposed to sideways, backwards, round in circles, we dropped anchor and started to fish.

Fishing from a boat – particularly the ease with which you can up and change swims at a moment's notice without having to pack all the gear away and carry it – does have a great deal in its favour. After ten minutes of not having any bites, the attraction of all the other completely deserted areas on the broad got the better of us, so we pulled up the anchor and moved off to other, equally fishless spots. After a while it became obvious that we were having so much fun just rowing around or drifting, looking over the side of the boat at the lake bottom and watching beds of cabbages and swan-mussels pass by, that this is exactly what we did for the rest of the afternoon. We had a great time and I don't remember seeing one fish.

By evening we'd become quite proficient at rowing the boat, but that was the last time we visited Rollesby Broad. Quite simply, the lack of fish found on the broad, and the wealth of other fisheries we had at our disposal, meant we could constantly move to new places. We were that spoilt for choice.

The next day was spent leisurely fishing one of the many rivers in the area, talking to various local anglers and getting information from the main tackle dealer, Ken Latham's in Potter Heigham. We made frequent trips back there during the two-week holiday, getting bait and ever more information regarding the type of fishing we enjoyed most, and this enabled us to sniff out a few nice places to try. As a generalisation, if we fished during the day, we grabbed a few hours' sleep at night, then were up early again the following morning for another day's fishing. If we night fished, however, we tended to lose a good few hours of day-time fishing.

One of our most memorable sessions came at night. We were fishing at Deep Dyke, an area situated at the far end of Hickling Broad. We'd been told that the bream fishing was good in this area, so one fine sunny day we loaded the car and set out for Hickling. On arrival at the boatyard, we were given a boat with an outboard and pointed in the direction of Deep Dyke, seemingly a million miles away up the other end of the Broad. 'Just keep going till the water narrows. That's Deep Dyke.'

After what seemed an age of being buffeted by twinkly sparkling waves, we saw that the Broad finally did begin to narrow and we found ourselves travelling up what was presumably Deep Dyke. There were a few house-boats moored on the opposite bank, but we chugged quietly along this area until we found a deserted spot which was to our liking, and we pulled in and moored. The banks were grassy, nice and flat, though somewhat eroded through constant wave action, but very comfortable to fish and low to the water. The river at this point was about thirty-five yards wide, with a narrow band of reeds on the far bank, and with fields beyond. Immediately behind us was the largest expanse of reeds we'd ever seen, stretching as far into the distance as we could make out. In hindsight, I think maybe the easiest way to have fished it would have been to ledger the swim in some way, but because we were both so fond of watching long white peacock quills in a torch beam at the time, this is how we tackled it.

We both set up match rods and Mitchell reels, plumbed the areas immediately in front and around us, and endeavoured to fish as far out as we could comfortably manage with the peacock quills. These we fished with baits laid heavily on the bottom, directly out in front of us, about midway out in the channel. If I remember rightly, we were using bunches of maggots and bread cocktails. We groundbaited heavily, preparing for the evening and night session, hoping for a large catch of bream, which as it turned out, didn't really materialise. But we had great fun. We ate endless bags of salt-and-vinegar crisps and drank bottles of cherryade, and caught a few bream to around four or five pounds. The bites showed up wonderfully well in the torch beams shining across the water, skimming the surface onto the brilliant white peacock quills: little dips, long lazy lifts, teetering for a couple of seconds, then definite slide-aways as the floats cut under the surface. It was (and is) a magical way of fishing. The match rods would hoop over to that wonderful sullen thump of a large bream far out in the drag of the current in the darkness. On a long line in a deep pulling current, bream on light tackle are quite simply intoxicating. In the dead of night, with myriads of insects skating in and out of a long-raking torch beam cutting across a deserted waterway, with sedge warblers chattering behind you, and your bream breaking surface coming to net, that big bronze flank catching in the remaining light… there really isn't anything to match it.

At one point, when the evening breeze had died down, probably around midnight, we noticed a wake of ripples heading upstream, bisecting our two floats. As we watched and followed it with the torch beams, we could see the massive head of a coypu cruising through the swim. Its head was the size of a bucket. We eventually lost sight of it as it made its way upriver. A little later in the early hours of the morning we heard it, or perhaps another one, crashing around in the reeds just behind us. If you didn't know what was making all that noise, you'd be excused for thinking someone was trying to force their way through the undergrowth with a wheelbarrow.

As the night wore on, things began to take their toll. The crisps and cherryade began to combine and do pretty nasty things to my stomach.

Since we were so close to the reeds, the area must have been a breeding ground for mosquitoes and, for some reason, horseflies.

We wanted to stay awake all night so that we could watch the floats. Vince kept nodding off, napping in his chair for ten minutes at a time, but I was kept awake by my churning stomach. Because of my restlessness I managed to keep moving enough to swat off the mosquitoes when they landed on me. By morning, although we had caught a few bream, we were both wrecks. Vince, on seeing the state I was in, kindly suggested we go back to the room, but it was all I could do to disappear into the reeds and throw up everything I'd drunk and eaten the evening before. After I'd done that I felt fine… except for feeling completely dead. Meanwhile, Vince had begun to count the horsefly bites and had to give up when the tally became too frightening to contemplate. He had eighteen on his forehead alone.

With sunrise, and the freshness of a new morning, we found it in ourselves to fish on for a few more hours and caught several nice roach. It never ceases to amaze me that no matter how tired one can be, there comes a time when there seems to be a rejuvenation of sorts. This can last a few hours, and can be quite exhilarating in fact, but then the inevitable need for sleep takes hold. In my case, when I reach this point, I find that if I close my eyes for longer than a blink, I start to dream. These dreams last mere seconds. I re-open my eyes, only to close them again – and start a new dream immediately. This can go on for as long as it takes for me to completely black out, no matter where I am.

For the next few days we dithered around the Martham area, fishing the River Thurne at night. I had fun with the eels, while Vince did everything he could to avoid them. During the days we fished Martham Ponds, but in the main left the fish in peace save for the odd small bream, tench and eel. I'd read in an old book somewhere that a good way of persuading an eel to calm down was to cut a long groove in the bank and on capturing one, somehow place it upside down within this groove as straight as you could manage. Intrigued by the thought of coercing an eel into anything approaching straightness, and with the groove duly chiselled out in the bank beside me, I awaited the next bite. The eel, still on the hook and weighing nearly two pounds, was given the groove-treatment, in the hope that this would calm it down long enough for me to unhook it without the usual circus act. Carefully, almost lovingly, I coaxed the eel into the groove on the bank, whereupon it just lay there, stiff as a bank stick. We stood back and admired it. For several minutes I honestly thought I'd killed it. I picked it up, unhooked it, and held it by the neck where it hung completely limp and apparently lifeless. Feeling awful, I was just about to look round for somewhere to bury it, when the eel woke from its hypnotic state and proceeded to do what all good eels do – attempting to lever my arm out of its socket, whilst at the same time, covering me in slime from head to foot, before skydiving back into the pond.

The morning of Wednesday, August 17th, found us sitting at the breakfast table trying to hold a conversation with two families of anglers. I suspect that Vince managed it better than I. Although in most circumstances I can strike up a conversation with a dead cat, when I'm trying to do it while in a state akin to that of the hypnotized eel through lack of sleep I find myself staring into space, looking through walls and generally falling asleep while I'm attempting to talk. The wife of the owner came into the room with the news…

'Elvis is dead.'

Vince and I, being great Elvis fans, responded in our usual off-the-wall manner. In our exhausted state we were probably even sillier than normal, and it wasn't until she slapped the morning paper on the table that we realised she wasn't joking.

It was on that day that we decided to look round the Potter Heigham area on the River Bure, with a view to night fishing the river for bream later that evening. A stop-off at Latham's for bait and more salt and vinegar crisps (washed down this time with a bucket load of Tizer), and we were armed with the essentials of life. We parked, and then went for a walk along the river. It really did look fabulous. The path we walked along ran through what was almost an impenetrable jungle of reeds. I'd never seen reeds so high before; I've never seen such high reeds since. I thought that this is what it must have been like, walking through bamboo forests in China. I could almost imagine pushing apart the reeds and tripping over pandas instead of coypus. Well above head height, the reeds blotted out any light from above, and in fishing terms, formed a wonderful backdrop and windbreak behind us. At intervals along the way, swims had previously been cut or flattened out by enterprising anglers, and the water was lovely and still, very dark. It looked so inviting and fishy I just wanted to dive in and throw bream onto the bank. We didn't need to convince each other any further: we had to turn round, jump into the car, speed back to get the gear and return as quickly as possible.

It wasn't too long before we were both set up in a wonderfully secluded spot, hemmed in on all sides by reeds giving on to more reeds. The water looked perfect, just as before, calm and still, and although the odd boat passed by further out, we felt sure we were bound to catch fish after fish.

The place was a haven for warblers, incessantly chattering around us;

dragonflies lazily skimmed around in front of our swim and perched on our peacock quills. We fished as we did at Deep Dyke: six-inch quills laid hard on the bottom with two or three BBs, size 8 spade-ends, and bunches of maggot and flake cocktails. I seem to remember the water being quite deep. Once we'd got the groundbait out we sat back and began somehow to inhale the day, not wishing it to end. This was definitely one of those Sixpence Jar Moments.

After a while the water began to draw terribly and for a moment I wondered what the hell was going on. Of course, it was tidal at this point, and we'd arrived at the time when the tide had been at its lowest. Now the current began to pull. I suppose we must have experienced the same thing on other rivers during our fortnight's holiday, but never a draw such as this. This one really meant it, and a drastic re-think on how we were now going to tackle the swim was called for. Furthermore the light was closing in and the weather seemed to be changing for the worse. Things seemed to be getting out of hand. Even the warblers had stopped singing. This alone didn't bode well. The current was really dragging by now and I'd gone through several tackle changes, none of which helped at all. I finally ended up tying together three ¼oz Arlesey bombs and ledgering, but by the time the leads found anywhere to rest they'd lodged directly downstream of me, to my right, with the rod tip pulling over and the bait about a foot from the bank.

At some time during the dark hours the wind picked up and the rain arrived – sheets of it. We piled in the groundbait and for a while, the bream moved in. I had bite after bite, the rod tip on my match rod pulling hard over. The shoal must have been right under my feet. Admittedly some of these must have been 'line bites', because as soon as I dropped in a big piece of flake, the rod tip would nod a few times and pull right round. Inexplicably, on three consecutive drops, I connected with three bream, all just under four pounds, and then went back to missing more and more of them. Playing a bream on light tackle in the heavy current was pretty exciting stuff, but after a while it seemed the shoal must have passed through. The groundbait must have all washed through to my side, since Vince, fishing only slightly upstream of me, had found it no good at all. He just folded his umbrella around himself and slept through it all.

By dawn the rain left off and the sun broke through, leaving us with a lovely day in prospect. A houseboat moored immediately downstream of us, and a family came out to stretch their legs. During their stop-off, the children, a little boy and girl aged about seven or eight, adopted us for an hour or two and wouldn't leave us alone, me in particular. I was barraged with questions, none of which I can now recall – although I do remember being constantly bashed over the head with a Snoopy doll.

We gave ourselves and all our tackle a suitable time to dry out, then packed everything away nice and dry. We'd completely forgotten, of course, the walk back through the Chinese bamboo forest, and by the time we reached the car we were absolutely soaked through again.

We crawled back into the room, whereupon it was all I could do to launch myself onto the bed, spiders or no spiders, and instantly fall asleep…

'Mole… Mole… I've smashed the car.'

'What?'

'I've smashed the car…'

I was being shaken awake by a lunatic. Only one second had gone by since I'd closed my eyes, and now I was being shaken to pieces by a maniac.

The truth? Vince had slept, woken and written a letter to his mum and gone out in the car to post it, while I slept on. It was while he was turning into the car park of a pub near the local post office when someone came speeding along an approach road and smashed into his left rear wing.

And that was our Norfolk holiday. Between the electric shock and the smashed car lie all those memories of the fun, the company, coypus crashing through the reeds, Elvis leaving the building permanently, and of course the fish; in particular the three bream I had that night on the Bure, while Vince was sleeping in his own umbrella.

PAINT IT BLACK

I was fishing alone – pike fishing, sitting behind two rods at the Railway Pit in Turnford. I'd been fishing since first light, and by now I was getting a little bored with my own company and watching the coots fight (they'd been scrapping since dawn). As I looked past my lines, my gaze took in a movement on the far bank. It was a black cat. I couldn't honestly remember if seeing a black cat was meant to be good luck or bad, but at that precise moment my indicator lifted and I hooked and landed my best pike from that lake: 16lb 2oz. Whatever the origins of the superstition, a black cat was now, for me, good luck.

On my next trip, I saw a black cat with some white on it.

I had some good luck on that day, but it was also tainted with some bad luck, i.e. white bits. I was now stuck with this awful portent every time I went fishing. Almost without exception, looking back, if I have had a bad day, or a day with an amount of bad luck, then without doubt, the first cat I'll have seen on the way to that particular fishery will have been a black and white one. It's got to the point now that if I see such a cat, I will expect to hook a fabulous fish but will probably have it fall off at the net as the bad luck kicks in.

I can recall dozens of instances of seeing these wretched things on the way to fisheries, but the most memorable must surely have been on the day I went to fish Friday Lake on Friday the Thirteenth. My good mate Bob Jermy and I pulled up in the car park, and I'd got out and was now standing behind the back of his car, rejoicing in the fact that we'd made it to the lake without having seen even one black and white cat. As I leant back, hands behind my head, having a good stretch, I looked down and the biggest fluffiest black and white pussy I'd ever seen calmly walked out from under the car, looked up at me, and walked off without the slightest care in the world. It was almost enough for me to make Bob turn round and drive me home.

We never had a bite.

The biggest laugh of all came over twenty-five years later when I decided to return to fish the same Railway Pit with Scotty. Recounting the Friday the Thirteenth story on the way down in the car, we pulled up in the car-park at the end of the lane. Leaving the car there, we both walked back to the same swim where all this nonsense began all those years ago. On deciding we'd give the swim a go for old times' sake, Scotty backed the car up and we unloaded the gear. He then drove back to the car-park and left me with all the tackle. I stood there having a preliminary stretch. At that precise moment, I heard a loud meowing, and from beneath a load of fallen branches out walked a black and white cat. He became our constant friend over three trips, during which we fed him half our dead-baits and sandwiches.

But no fish.

HOOKED ON PIKE

While I write, I can see the mists forming in front of me, whitening everything out, and I can feel the morning cooling as it swirls quietly before me. As the mist soundlessly begins to clear I can make out these two same hands, my hands, as I press my line into the slit in the small red-tipped Fishing Gazette float.

There was something quite magical in the lead up to the first cast of a day spent searching for pike when I was thirteen. Arriving at the gravel pit at Admiral's Walk, and invariably walking up to that first little reedy corner; getting the five foot, white spinning rod out of the bag; setting up the Mitchell 314; threading the line through the rings and tying on the trace with the one size 8 treble. But the moment that held all those moments together was the putting on of that float – the putting on of that float with the special slit in the side, and pressing the peg in to secure it at the right depth: four feet, since this was the deepest I could comfortably set it to cast.

Two feet was too shallow. One foot was ridiculous. Three feet was so-so, but I was never happy with it, and I could never imagine any pike worth its spots swimming so near to the surface. And anyway, I wasn't happy if I could see my sprat dangling and glittering underneath the float. The fishing would have no mystery to it if I could see the bait. Five feet and I couldn't cast properly. I tried several times and managed on most of them to fling off my sprats, which invariably landed in the water rather than on the bank, where at least I could have retrieved them. So four feet it was then – a good, manageable fishing depth. I could cast reasonably well with the float plugged at that depth, and I couldn't see the sprat when it settled. Perfect.

All subsequent pike caught by Mr. Pledger, ace pike-catcher supreme of Hoddesdon, would accordingly have to be swimming at four feet depth – by law.

Pete and I would fish away in the same spots and we never tired of or changed our methods. A pound-and-a-half of sprats bought from Brewster's (the fishmonger in Hoddesdon), a few pike traces, a couple of spare floats, a landing net – and that was it. Some days we caught pike, some days we didn't. We caught nothing larger than my fabled beauty of 5lb 8oz – a fish whose capture was so often, and so imaginatively, re-told – which in turn superseded the one of 4lb 8oz which had remained my heaviest for so long that I thought I would be sporting a beard to rival Darwin's before I bettered it.

And so the mists roll in, and then start to clear. And as they clear once again, I find it's September 20th, 1970 – a day that gave my limping interest in pike a little nudge in the back. I'd gone back to re-visit Admiral's Walk with a couple of schoolmates one afternoon, and using the same rod and reel I always used, cast out a dead three-inch roach a few yards along from my favourite corner. I remember I was using a sliding porcupine quill, and fished the bait on a single hook straight through to 7lb line with no trace, tight on the bottom. I placed the bait against an overhanging willow bush, which was growing on a spit of land surrounded by reeds.

It was a twenty-yard cast, made directly in front of me. Within a few minutes the float slowly cocked, twitched a few times and glided under to the right. Glancing back to my line I could see a bow, as if caused by a right-to-left breeze, gently being taken out as I opened the bail arm. I let the pike take a couple of yards, closed the bail arm and pulled into the fish, which immediately suggested to me it was neither 4lb 8oz, 5lb 8oz, or anywhere near wanting to come over to say hello. For several minutes it did whatever it wanted, with me just hanging on in disbelief. Finally, I must have done everything exactly right, and it did come over to say hello. It was the largest pike I had ever seen. Weighed at 13lb 8oz, its capture was to become my often, really very very often-repeated pike story for quite some time, and I think even I may have tired of repeating the tale to myself before I finally came to catch a pike which bettered it.

Pike seemed to become increasingly difficult to catch the more I began to think about it. As I mentioned before, on more trips than I care to remember, all I ever did was suspend my sprat four feet down in the vicinity of some nice reeds. My thinking never went beyond this and the pike seemed quite happy with this default tactic. Then I began to read books on pike fishing, and my young mind was awash with countless diagrams of rigs and methods, descriptions of optimum feeding times, best places to fish, water temperatures, clarity and depth of water, flow in rivers, best baits in autumn, even better baits in winter, and so on… and so on…

This had the effect that if I sat there for more than thirty minutes with nothing happening then my mind would go into overdrive as I tried to puzzle out what I was doing wrong. Previously, my only thought on the matter would have been that my lack of success was simply because there were no pike present. Post-pike-reading, however, and my mind would now be in a turmoil. Was the water, or the day, too cold or too hot? Was it too windy – or not windy enough? Was the bait fishing too deep or too shallow? Was the flow too fast or not fast enough? And if and but and maybe and maybe not – in the end I'd just get the fidgets – I'd read too many books.

What became my 'normal' method would generally be to free-line a sprat or half a herring on the bottom of the lake or river, with as little lead on the line as I thought necessary – this usually being nothing more than a swanshot or two about two feet up the line from the trace. Once the bait and weight had been lightly flicked out, I'd place a plastic wine bottle top over the line in front of the Mitchell 410, with the bail arm left open. I loved to watch the first indications of the bottle top as it twitched and slowly inched up, the line trickling off the spool as the bow from the rod tip pulled out and disappeared into the surface film. Sometimes, on a hesitant take, the line would stop, whereupon the pike could be induced to take again by gently pulling on the line and feeling for a reaction the other end. An otherwise half-interested pike could usually be cajoled into grabbing a sprat he'd previously dropped after having second thoughts. Once the line started to feed out from the rod tip again, in what was so often a more positive manner, it was a mere formality to close the bail arm, wait for the line to tighten and pull the rod sideways so that the pike, which was by now running off with the bait, was firmly hooked.

By the time pike had become annoying, given their habit of throwing me more questions than answers, I'd progressed beyond my little white spinning rod to a superb 10 foot hollow glass Dick Walker Mk IV Avon, sold to me by Mr. Ross in the tackle shop in Hoddesdon. I remember the day he quietly took me to one side, looked at me, smiled and said, 'Maurice… have I got a rod for you…' And by golly, he had. Usually he'd try to sell Scotty, Vince and myself anything he felt like – something that had no connection whatsoever with what we'd intended to buy that day. On paying for a pint of maggots, for example, we'd be offered a set of mackerel feathers. If we'd just bought half a dozen floats, some line and hooks, Mr. Ross would follow up the sale by asking if we'd like a bag of freshly caught ragworm. On this occasion though, Mr. Ross, even if on one of his eccentric benders, had it absolutely spot on. I wasn't really in need of a rod that particular morning, and my eyes were still wandering around the shelves and cabinets as Mr. Ross untied the rod bag. Imagining it to be yet another beachcaster he wanted to show me, in the mistaken idea that I was having afternoon tea with Leslie Moncrieff, my gaze soon fixed, in a kind of rapt adoration, on what I was going to be shortly walking out of the door with.

The more that Vince, Chad and myself fished for pike, the more it became obvious that the larger fish kept away from us. More often than we cared to admit the blank days outnumbered the good ones, and the good ones only yielded pike in small numbers and of a small average size. Then one day, for no reason at all, the clouds parted and the sun shone through.

We three found ourselves in Nazeing, at Heartbreak Pit which had been so-named because its fish weren't altogether keen to be caught by anybody, least of all by any of us. My two rods were set up at the bottom of a high, steeply sloping bank near the water's edge. Vince and Chad were fishing a little further along. We were all perched precariously on the top of this high bank, watching the indicators below. I noticed one of mine creep up and I very carefully inched my way down to deal with it, which I did in admirable fashion, and duly landed a lovely pike of 8lb 8oz. After I'd netted it I made my way to the top of the bank, unhooked and photographed the fish… and it was at this point it all came undone. On stepping back onto the slope with the pike in my arms, my legs gave way and I very neatly slid down the entire bank on my back, cradling the fish, watching the lake looming. I could do nothing to stop my flight downwards. Both pike and I hit the lake as one, the pike being the happier of the two of us, and after a minute or so of floundering and flannelling I crawled back out, utterly soaked through. I went home for a change of clothes, returned, baited up and cast out.

Unbelievably, the indicator rose again to a second run. This time my descent was as careful as I could make it. On pulling into the fish it immediately became obvious that this was one of Heartbreak's heart breakers, and it had no intention at all of coming anywhere near me. For what seemed like an eternity we went through the formalities that suggested to my unbelieving mates on the bank above that The Wet One had hooked into something rather special. As she rose in the water we began to make out a large crocodile-like shape looming towards us. After a few unstoppable surges into the bay in front of me she reluctantly turned, came back and I netted her. Fish and I made it to the top and back down again without repeating the earlier mishap. At 17lb 12oz she remained my heaviest pike for a long while – which is how it should be, because it gives you time enough to appreciate such special fish when they do show up on these rarest of rare occasions, and spurs you on to keep fishing through all the blank days which invariably outnumber the bountiful ones.

I've gone through periods of fishing a great deal with Vince, Scott and Chad, but also with another great friend of mine, Steve Tibble from Welwyn; Steve of the Great Turnip Saga. Steve, who is about a year older than me, was one of the lads who worked for my dad at the printing works and was introduced to me by Dad when he learnt that here was as besotted a fisherman as me. It was a foregone conclusion that we two, with Dad as the catalyst, would become the greatest of friends and we spent many seasons fishing together. From those earliest meetings our friendship augured well. Steve's sense of humour was as warped as mine, so it looked as though more fishing trips could and would be crammed in on top of all my usual ones. We both particularly liked chub and carp fishing, pike too. For many seasons we haunted the gravel pits around the Slipe Lane area in Turnford, particularly the large lake sitting alongside King's Weir, the Railway Pit at the end of Slipe Lane, and the large gravel pit a little further along, a place we simply called the Big Turnford Pit. We centred most of our activities on these three gravel pits during the autumn and winter during the late seventies and early eighties.

These three pits generated many trips and many memories. How many early autumn and winter pre-dawn starts we made I wouldn't care to guess – nor how many sprats, herrings and mackerel we hurled out, nor how many hours we sat behind the rods, waiting for the white plastic indicators to creep up. For me, the one delicious moment in deadbaiting for pike must surely be that first instance when the indicator twitches. You know with absolute and delicious certainty that a pike is sniffing around the bait, but at that moment you have no way of knowing whether it's a small jack or a pike you could put a saddle on. There! Just a twitch, nothing more, but the line is now alive and your senses are at their keenest… now the indicator hanging lifeless, wet and dripping, suspended a few inches above the muddy bank. The raindrops knock it gently, but then it twitches up half an inch. Against the rain, against the larger, heavier drops from the trees, another twitch… then it slowly creeps up towards the butt ring. In the games of sit and wait, there really is nothing like it.

I was now looking at my finger: the third finger in, counting from the thumb on my right hand. It had a size 8 treble-hook buried to the bend in the top of it. I was sitting, soaking wet, in the doctor's crowded waiting room on a bitterly cold, dismal winter's evening, with hail and sleet slashing into the windows. Forty people were looking directly at me. It was all I could do to get my boots off in the car, and because I couldn't get my shoes on (have you ever tried to pull on a pair of shoes with a treble embedded in a finger?), I'd walked through all the puddles in the car-park to the reception in my socks, which were now sodden. My finger had stopped bleeding a while ago, but now was dreadfully swollen, with the prong of the hook still disappearing into the flesh. I wondered how on earth the doctor would go about sorting it out. I'd entered Reception, tried in vain to sign my name in the book using an arm that had no feeling from the elbow down, and gingerly shouldered the door open into a room that looked like rush hour on the underground.

An hour previously I was in the middle of nowhere, on the Big Turnford Pit, trying to persuade a three-pound pike not to leap around like a frog in a frying pan. That was when the hook went into my finger. I'd been wobbling sprats on the bleakest of winter afternoons. I was soaked and frozen to the insides of my Barbour, which had decided to give up trying to protect me from the weather, when the pike took.

Trying to calm down a three-pound jumping firecracker with the loose prong of a treble jammed to the hilt in my finger wasn't proving easy. I couldn't see anything because of the mud I was skidding around in, and the sleet stung my face. In any case, I was crying. It took me at least five minutes to slither back to the tackle-box where I kept the scissors. Still hooked to the pike, I finally made it back to the scissors, when it became obvious I couldn't cut the trace using my left hand. Ten minutes later – a full fifteen minutes after the hook went in – I managed it, and returned the pike. Then there was a half-mile walk, leaning into sleet, back to the car, more leaning, then driving into sleet…

Back in the waiting room and I'm still staring at my finger.

'I'd imagine it's not going to be easy working, with that stuck in your finger.'

My eyes slowly lifted to an elderly lady sitting opposite, who was trying to strike up some kind of conversation. I was in no mood, but out of politeness went along with it.

'Funnily enough, you're right,' I said. 'I actually paint pictures of birds and animals, so this will probably hold me up a bit.'

Her face brightened.

'Oh, that's interesting. I know of an artist, a young gentleman. I've followed his work for many years. I collect his greeting cards. He paints the most marvellous birds and animals, too. His father's English and his mother's Italian.'

'Yes, that's me.'

She immediately got to her feet, walked over, grabbed my left arm with one hand and shoved her other one into my hand – the one with the hook in it.

'Well, I never! I want to shake your hand.'

At that point she sat back down, most pleased with things, and for a few seconds I went back to looking at my finger, trying not to cry again.

One of the receptionists, who hadn't seen me come in, and who hadn't been able to understand my attempted scrawl in the patients' book on arrival, put her head round the door to call the next patient through.

In a silent room, in a loud clear voice:

'Maureen Pledger…'

At which I got up and walked to the door, followed by forty pairs of raised eyebrows.

Unfortunately this little episode was replicated a year later (almost to the day, funnily enough), when I found myself walking through the same doctor's surgery door, on an equally cold wet and miserable evening, with yet another treble stuck firmly in the tip of the same finger. Almost unbelievably, the accident had happened in exactly the same way. On opening the outer door, and standing there, dripping, at the reception desk, I meekly held up my finger with the hook buried in it, looked at the nice lady at reception, and said:

'Remember me? Maureen…'

Maureen Pledger

M.J.PLEDGER

OUR BIGGEST PIKE

On September 9th, 1985 Scotty and I resumed our fishing together. Scott had moved away from Hoddesdon for what seemed interminable years searching for fame and fortune elsewhere. But from that auspicious date right up to the present, scarcely a week goes by without us arranging some fishing. For years, in the colder months we'd concentrate on pike fishing. The Big Pit at Turnford still drew our attention, as did (in particular) the smaller pit next to it, which we named Little Turnford. The two pits, and the pike in them, had completely different characters, and because we seemed to come to terms more easily with the pike in the smaller pit, we gave them more of our time.

Wormleybury, a private estate lake in Broxbourne, Toyhall, one of our club lakes in Cheshunt, and a series of gravel pits at Rye Meads near Hoddesdon also attracted our attention. In the main, our methods would be the same as those I've already mentioned, and looking back through all my notebooks, I suppose most of the larger pike came to dead baits fished static, with herrings or half herrings being the baits which seemed to interest the really big pike. It was from our love of photography, and of taking photos of the fish we caught, that we became aware that some of the same pike were being re-caught on subsequent trips. By carefully checking the markings of pike in our photos against those of previous captures, we began to note how some particular fish would either gain or lose weight over a period of time.

One friendly pike, a fish we named 'Yellowspot' because of a yellow marking on the underside of her jaw, was first caught by Scott. She weighed 17lb 6oz in the Little Turnford Pit on October 16th, 1985. I then caught her three times in quick succession on the 18th, 22nd and 29th September, 1986. She said hello to Scott again on October 21st. She took a completely different bait each time. On one occasion I'd previously found a dead jack of about a pound and a half in weight and decided on a whim to use it for bait. Because it was so heavy I had to throw it out by hand. As it slowly sank I could see the line trickling off the spool while it descended to the bottom in about six feet of water in a narrow little gully we called 'The Strip,' which lay just in front of my feet. After a few seconds it dawned on me that the jack should have already reached the bottom but the line was still slowly inching out. I realised that the bait had been picked up so I readied the landing net, closed the bail arm, and watched as the line pulled tight and curved the rod into a very surprised and irate pike. It was Yellowspot again, and as she drew towards the net I could just make out the extreme tail tips of the jack protruding from her closed mouth. When she was on the bank, I gently opened her mouth and slid the jack out; not one hook had caught hold. Quite simply, she just didn't want to let go.

One little ruse Scott and I delighted in resorting to whenever the fishing was really slow was cannonading the immediate area around the baits with stones and bricks. Of course, this was always done when no-one else was around, so if we had the general area (or even better, the whole lake) to ourselves, we'd take it in turns to go off and hunt for a few armfuls of bricks, the bigger the better. We'd read somewhere of someone scaring uninterested pike out of some bankside reeds, whereupon the disturbance woke them up enough to start them taking a few baits. On the first occasion we tried this we thought we had nothing to lose and so in went the bricks. Indeed, we caught a few pike, either despite the disturbance or because of it. No matter, on every subsequent trip, whether we were catching pike or not, we needed no excuse to go ahead and give each other's baits a good cataclysmic pounding. In fact, fifteen minutes prior to my catching a beautiful pike of 22lb 4oz in a secluded little area we called 'Back Bays' in Little Turnford, I'd been dropping several half bricks around my float, from which a whole herring was suspended.

Such was this yearning to catch pike that Scott and I drifted into a series of trips night fishing for them. We'd noticed time and again that late afternoon in winter seemed to be the start of a second or third feeding spree. Since dusk generally coincided with us packing up, we decided to arrive for our fishing in the afternoon and fish on until quite late, in the hope that the more wary larger pike might lose some of their caution in the hours of darkness. Although we did catch several decent fish, the big ones didn't show up as we expected. We just experienced more tangles than usual, kicked over more tackle boxes, and generally enjoyed ourselves no end.

The culmination of all this came on the evening of October 15th, 1987. We set out to fish Toyhall, our club lake which bordered the North Met Pit, chosing to fish a deep area of the lake, the scene of many previous pike captures. We arrived at 7 p.m. By about nine things had got decidedly windy, and like the pair of idiots we are, we still sat together under our umbrellas facing directly into the teeth of this strengthening gale. Only after two hours of this farce did we think of turning the umbrellas round so that we'd have the gale at our backs. By ten thirty we decided we'd had enough, since by then the wind really was cranking it up, so we packed in and left for home. From the newspapers and news reports the following morning, we found out that we had actually been out fishing in what was to become know as the Great Hurricane. It had flattened half the country.

If the hurricane wasn't enough to dent our enthusiasm for pike fishing, not even severe winters and freeze-ups managed it either. A memorable trip on the last day of the season, once again at Wormleybury, saw us smashing holes in ice so thick you could walk on it. We hurled out a brick tied to a length of washing line, and continually crashed the edges off the ice close in to the bank in only two feet of water. After we'd got the sprats into the water, and literally only fifteen feet out, we started catching small pike of up to three pounds. Within only five or ten minutes of the most appalling crashing and splashing, we'd begun to get runs on our baits. Because it was so cold, you could actually watch the ice re-forming along the edge of a hole, while any ice-free hole would close up completely within thirty minutes. We had to continually hurl out the ice-breaker, and following the onslaught, and on some occasions within seconds, we were back catching more pike.

It was at Wormleybury, on January 20th, 1986, where I had one of my weirdest incidents with pike. I'd arrived on my own on a grey, gloomy day and had decided to fish from the wooded bank. I set up three rods, two of which were light Avons, and cast buoyant sprats over to the fringe of dead lilies bordering the bank at the other side of the lake about forty yards away. On the third rod I free-lined a herring close in to my right, alongside a line of reeds running towards a dead tree that had fallen into the lake.

Until this point, all the pike we'd caught from that spot were usually in the two to four pound range, with the odd one slightly heavier. There was rumoured to be one very large pike in the lake, a monster fish of over twenty pounds, but with every new three-pounder landed, this story wore a little thinner. Because the lake was nowhere much deeper than three feet, the buoyant sprats must have been floating within a foot of the surface. The Wormleybury pike seemed to enjoy this.

M.J.PLEDGER.

From the start I could see it was going to be one of those good days, with twitches, takes, runs and indeed, pike, coming to all three rods with a frequency that had me fussing around like an old mother hen. At twenty past twelve the sprat on the middle rod was seized. The line simply hissed off the spool in a blur. In fact even when I picked up the rod, attempted to close the bail arm, failed a couple of times, and finally managed it, the Optonic was still howling. The rod took on a curve and nearly left to join the immense swirl about sixty yards down the lake. The fish cut right across into my bank and ploughed straight into the dead tree. There was nothing I could do but hang on and watch. I'd resigned myself to waving the fish goodbye, and of at least having the privilege of knowing that the giant pike of Wormleybury was not a fairy tale.

I could see, out there on a long line, a large back half-in and half-out of the water, all tangled in the branches while the pike careened about, sending every moorhen and coot in the district skittering in alarm across the lake. I simply held on and hoped that something would kick free. Then against all hope I began to win back some line on the Mitchell and the swirls and troughs in the water rocked nearer and nearer. Free from the dead branches, the pike was now heading my way. I still couldn't coerce this fish into moving out into the main lake as it nose-dived straight into and through the old bankside reeds. I think Fate may have been somewhere else – playing cards with a black and white cat perhaps – because all my luck held and agonisingly slowly, what became known as 'The Legend' came nearer… and nearer...

Presently the fish was under the rod tip. Incredibly, and in only three feet of water, I still could not lift the pike from the bottom, and with the rod fully arched over and the fish circling and swirling at my feet I began to wonder just how big it was. Old dead leaves from season on season of accumulated silt churned and wafted up amongst the vortexes as the fish stubbornly refused to be brought up from the margins. Several times I managed to gain a foot of line, only to have the rod tip jar back down, but eventually I drew the fish slowly to the surface.

I placed the net ready and slowly the fish lifted from within all the swirling silt in front of me…

Hooked fairly in the middle of the bottom lip, with the sprat still hanging alongside, was an enormous mirror carp of 20lb 10oz – my biggest Wormleybury pike.

OUR BIGGEST PIKE

Rye Meads is a series of gravel pits nestling in the country between the outskirts of Hoddesdon and Roydon. I used to go birdwatching around this area with Dad when I was nine or ten, before the pits had been excavated. When Vince, Chad and I were fifteen we used to fish the area, which was still just a meandering little River Stort winding its way through fields. Such was our love for the place, one of us named it the Stort Reject. Some years later the pits were dug out, became established and naturalised, and then completely overgrown (especially with willows and sallows), and somehow or other whatever fish were in there began to grow, and grow. It wasn't until the place had really taken on the look of the Florida Everglades that Scott, Dave and I returned to fish. Sometimes, when I could manage to drag him down there, Vince came too.

At first we fished for tench, but as the winters came along we naturally began to draw the pike rods from our bags. Initially, during the first few trips we fished around a bit, then we ended up concentrating on a long narrow lake near the tollgate road. Here we fished what we famously named the 'Swan Swim', and had many memorable trips fishing side-by-side, free-lining herrings, catching numerous pike to just over fifteen pounds. Because the water levels were prone to rising and falling at a moment's notice on these pits it was quite strange to see grass 'growing' underwater as the banks gently shelved off. Of course the grass wasn't actually growing but, as the water levels rose so quickly over a period of days, it just seemed that way. The pike loved to lie in this long grass right in the edge, and several times large fish cruised quietly in, completely unnoticed, and lie by our feet. It was only as we got up to stretch our legs that a great swirl would herald a very large pike bolting off into deeper water.

I remember that on one particular day (Monday, March 2nd, 1987) in the Swan Swim, Scott caught a pike of 16lb 12oz. Before he could return it I also had a run, and landed one of 13lb 12oz. Because the brace of pike looked so wonderful I had the idea of keeping them for a while to show my children, Douglas and Laura, who were then respectively seven and three.

So when we packed up in the early afternoon, we left both fish comfortably in a sack hidden in the water. Scott dropped me off home, I collected Laura and we raced off to rescue Douglas, who was still in his last lesson of the day at primary school. I walked into his classroom and asked the teacher if Douglas could be excused because he had a dentist's appointment. Of course his teacher agreed, albeit in the middle of the lesson, and I dragged a surprised Douglas off. On the one mile trip back to Rye Meads the gasket blew on the car and smoke started belching from under the bonnet. We just made it to the lakes, and I proudly took photos of the pair of them standing with the two pike and then watched as we gently released the fish back into the water. We then had to return to the Fireball XL5 and only just made it home, wreathed in billowing clouds of smoke.

On Sunday, March 28th, 1988, for some reason I couldn't go fishing. Scott went along to Rye Meads with Clive, another friend of his, and fished along the deep bank of the last pit on the complex. This bank ran parallel to the little River Stort, whose course was diverted all those years ago and which now runs in a straight line alongside the lakes. The bank where Scott and Clive chose to fish, with the Stort at their backs, was very high and sloped steeply down to the water's edge where they set up their rods. The water close in along this bank was remarkably deep – a great contrast to the opposite bank forty yards away, which had more features and a shallow bar running along its course a couple of rod-lengths out.

I sat at home. The time came and went when Scott really should have phoned to say how they'd both got on. Time passed and I began to fidget. Then I phoned Scott at home, expecting him to be still out fishing. His wife,

Liz answered. 'Oh, he's been back hours. I'll go and get him.'

I thought this strange; normally Scott would have phoned me the moment he got back. He came to the phone, and without too much drama, in a more-or-less-couldn't-be-bothered kind of way, described the morning's events. Really dragging it out, he eventually told me of a fish whose size I was reluctant to believe.

As the story went, Scott, fishing in the deep water close in, was ledgering a whole herring which had air injected into it to make it buoyant. He'd had a run and latched into something which stayed deep for nearly ten minutes. During this time, a regurgitated tench came floating to the surface – a fish which, when alive, must have weighed in the region of two pounds. Of course, this added to the mystery of the unseen beast, but eventually the pike was landed and weighed 26lb 12oz. Because Scott hadn't phoned me immediately he really didn't convince me, and I allowed myself a few days' disbelieving grace until he got the photos developed.

Scott, Clive and I returned the next day but the weather was closing in fast, and in bitterly cold conditions none of us had a run. During the week I went round to Scott's to see the photos, and it was only then that I was convinced that he indeed did catch the pike of a lifetime.

The following Sunday saw us again in the same swims, eager as ever. At 7 a.m. Scott pulled out of a large pike which had taken a buoyant ledgered mackerel. The teeth marks left on the bait were four inches across and seemed to indicate a large fish. Fifteen minutes later I caught a pike of 8lb 5oz on a wobbled roach, then at ten thirty had a quiet take on a whole mackerel which I'd dropped right under my feet. My rod curved over into an incredibly heavy fish which came to the net reasonably quickly. Weighing 25lb 12oz, it was the same pike Scott had caught the previous Sunday. As the photographs confirmed, one of the pectoral fins was slightly smaller than the other – there was no question that it was the same fish. We named her Debbie. To this day she represents for each of us our personal best… our biggest pike.

OF TROUT AND KOOKABURRAS

More than fifteen years ago, I made friends with a lovely couple slightly older than me, John and Di Morwood. Jonno, born in Newcastle, had emigrated to Tasmania and had there met and eventually married his lovely wife. Fifteen years ago, and with their three young girls all still at school, John and Di made room for me to stay on three occasions at their spacious home in Launceston. My stays were spread over three years. The first lasted a week, and thereafter, in the following two years, I enjoyed trips of three weeks each. It was during these stays that I became intoxicated with the Tassie people and their way of life – their laid-back attitude, the incredible countryside, the wonderful brown trout fishing, the family's close mates, John and Bev… and Freddo. Freddo (Fred Lunstroo) is the most completely off-the-wall nut-case and all-round number one nice guy. John and Fred were inseparable fishing companions.

It was always a sad day when I had to board the plane for home.

The fishing trips were fabulous. We made frequent short excursions to John and Fred's favourite local fishing patches: to Brumby's Creek, and to the tiny intimate stream, Lake River, and further afield to Penstock Lagoon and Lake Leake. There was an infinite variety of birds which we spotted along the banks: tiny spotted pardalotes, superb blue wrens, and grey fantails were my favourites, but it would take a page to list all the species which make up the wonderful patchwork of life there. Marsh harriers wheeled across the distances while a great flurry of sulphur-crested cockatoos would burst through the trees, setting off laughing kookaburras. If you diligently followed a kookaburra's raucous cry, you would invariably find him, sitting like a huge shrike atop an old bleached telegraph pole.

Watching John and Fred quietly stalk tailing wild brown trout along the flooding grassy edges of streams, with wand-like fly rods and three-weight lines, was like watching a poem being written. It was also lovely to see their respect for the wild, and their policy of catch and release.

Among many memorable trips, one particular afternoon stands out. Jonno and I were ambling along the delightful little Lake River. It was completely overgrown with overhanging bushes, gum trees, reeds and sunken dead wood. We were searching for any signs of small wild brownies. It was a warm, sunny day, quite sultry, with not much wind. Birds were singing, trees were in full leaf: it was truly lovely. We'd had a few small fish and were walking upstream when we reached a point where the thick growth of bankside tea tree bushes grew into the water. The banks at this point were three feet high and made of clay. In previous weeks, the water had been high but had now fined down and cleared, dropping back to normal height.

Approaching the bushes, we both noticed a horrible, wafting smell of something long dead. It persisted for some yards, suggesting that whatever was causing the smell was probably in, or very close to, that spot. We couldn't find anything and reasoned that whatever it was must have been washed along in the current. Fortunately – or otherwise – we then noticed the water gently rocking under the overhanging tea tree leaves. Quietly watching, we spotted a couple of brownies rising up in the water, becoming partly visible like materialising ghosts in flickering shafts of sunlight which were filtering into the water through the leaves. One looked to be around a pound while the other was a fair bit larger – a good Lake River fish. Jonno left me with the challenge as the smell was just too overpowering for him. I too had to keep leaving the spot briefly, but as there were no other fish around I kept returning, tying a handkerchief around my face to help mask the smell. Sometimes the trout were there, sometimes they weren't. Mostly they were. Directly under my feet there was a gaping hole in the clay bank with old tree roots protruding. The water ran three feet below, leaving just enough room to wiggle the rod tip through and dangle a dry fly on what were no more than two feet of line. My idea was that if I waited long enough maybe one of the brownies would rise and take the struggling fly as I jiggled it around.

It was while I was looking down into the water that I noticed something moving – something unnatural, but moving. Something weird. As I looked, it became slowly apparent that it was a big circular hole about the size of a big dinner plate – and yes, it was moving. I looked, then looked again, and I realised that what I was looking at was a heaving mass of maggots.

At this point, cogs began whirring and clicking, my eye wandered from this dinner plate of a million maggots, and it became clear that what I was actually looking at was the bleached carcass of a stranded, long-dead sheep. The dinner plate was in effect a large gape in the thigh of this poor unfortunate animal, which had obviously met its sorry end wedged under the bush and was now resting right on the edge of the waterline, covered in grey silt and bleaching in the sunshine. It was perfectly camouflaged; no wonder neither of us had seen it. The larger trout, around two-and-a-half pounds, had learned that if he rose in the water and gave the sheep a whack on its side with his nose, he could dislodge a couple of maggots at a time. They'd drop in and he'd quietly swirl and pick them up at his leisure. This rocking of the water is what we initially noticed as we walked upstream.

Jonno and I pondered a while. After fiddling through his fly box, he picked out an old fly tied to resemble a maggot. It was nothing more than a few turns of white wool wrapped around the shank of a hook. This he tied on and dangled over the side of the bank, next to the dinner plate. Within seconds, the rod tip nodded over and the smaller of the two fish unceremoniously came splashing ashore. We shot some video footage of the capture, additional photos were taken, and the brownie was returned to grow as big as his brother. It goes to show what a fish will do in a certain situation if it's left in peace long enough to work things out. Obviously the maggots were dropping over the lip of the hole now and then, but this trout was actually butting the side of the carcass to speed things up a bit.

Tasmania is a wonderful country and has left me with so many memories shared with delightful friends. Memories now safely stored in that old sixpence jar.

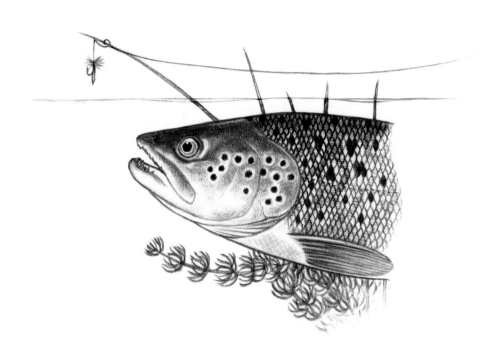

A THEATRE OF PERCH

Over thirty-five years have slipped off the reel since that big Homersfield perch hit the landing net. I remember the day as clearly as if it had happened this morning. Sitting at the foot of that monstrously high bank, the crest of which rose forty feet above me, and with water lapping at my feet, the first cast must have dropped the lobworm smack in the middle of a shoal of perch. The peacock quill settled, dipped and sailed away; it was all so easy. Perch after perch hit the net and they were all good fish, with none under twelve ounces and the best just short of two pounds. Somewhere among the proceedings, the float dipped as it had done so many times before and I found myself attached to an unseen fish which was far heavier. As it slowly thudded and kicked to the surface, I prayed for the hook to hold. Seeming indignant, the perch slid into the net. At 3lb 6oz, it dwarfed every perch I'd caught before.

After a while, to change the routine, I wandered off to try and catch a few more on a tiny Mepps spinner. Incredibly, that was to be my last successful day's perch fishing on a stillwater until 2008. In the intervening years, perch have come to my rod on the odd occasion, but rather by accident than by design, and only in running water.

In the early years, the nearest I came to thinking I had the measure of perch was on Hertford's little River Rib, on the bend before it joins with the Beane. As always during this period, I wandered the banks flicking out my customary lobworms using the tiny little eight-foot Ribtickler and a Mitchell 408. I'd previously found a secluded area under a great willow, its sprawling leafy branches creating a natural shady canopy, and I think fish of all kinds must have found the enclosed spot to their liking. On that prior trip I'd taken a couple of chub of around three and four pounds, and a wayward common carp of 5lb 14oz which led me a dance before I finally netted it. Of course, on the day in question I'd returned immediately to the same spot and had flicked the lobworm again under the branches. Bite indication was simple enough. I'd greased the line, and therefore all I needed to do to watch it as it lay in the surface film, cutting across a light area in the reflection of the sky. A take from a fish would register with the line appearing to have a tiny charge of electricity running through it. A little snick of the rod tip and the fish and I would be connected. Very few bites were missed.

And now I began to catch perch, one after the other, and of a very good size indeed. I had four or five, all between a pound and a pound-and-a-half. When I hit the next bite it immediately became obvious that I'd connected with my friend the carp of a previous visit since this fish just blundered about in the area like a sullen bull. In my haste to shorten the proceedings, and so as not to scare the perch shoal unduly, I tried to hustle the carp to the net. Yet when the fish finally rolled on the surface I realised that my supposed carp was in fact the sort of perch my mantelpiece had long dreamed of. I could feel myself somehow unhinge while I prayed each moment for the hook not to pull… I gasped every time the fish bored down, expecting it to find unseen snags – expecting it to throw the hook every time it surfaced and rolled. Finally, as I stretched with the net – almost overdoing the stretching and joining the fish in the river – the perch went in. Although I had no camera and no scales, it appeared to weigh a shade less than the Homersfield fish I'd recently caught, so I was happy to settle for a weight of three pounds as I gently released the fish there under the willow – a huge, small stream perch.

And that was it, I thought. The door to The Perch Room had now closed.

It isn't until around thirty-two years later that we can see a lonely figure already fishing at the weir. The date is October 14th, 2005, the figure is Vince, who is sitting in my favourite swim: No. 3 East, The Beach. It's ten in the morning and Vince is in the left hand side of the swim. He's already almost completed tackling up when I arrive. As always, he has left me enough room on his right, judging the distance by the distance he needs to lean to nab one of my scotch eggs.

The day started out as many others had at King's Weir over the years, but its events would thereafter dramatically affect all my fishing.

I'd taken along a delightful, roach-sized, ash wood landing net, shaped like a teardrop, with a two-piece, six-foot cane handle. It had been made in the 1930s, an exquisite little thing I'd bought from a friend, the frame of which measured only fifteen inches by twelve inches at its widest. I dearly wanted to christen the net, and told Vince he was to use it to land anything I caught. Because the ferrule on the handle was very loose we decided beforehand that it would probably be safer to use only one three foot section in case the full-length handle was to come adrift in any netting operation. Having settled on this and watching Vince trying out his new toy, practising infantile fly swatting movements with it, I began to question the logic in trusting him with a landing net that looked about as big as an Eskimo baby's snow-shoe. While he amused himself, I tackled up with my wand-like 10' 6" Drennan Bomb rod, a small fixed-spool reel and ultra-fine 6lb braid. As always I fished a very light running link-ledger with a 16" hook link, cast a large lobworm into the pool and bounced it all around the place. On a good day, and in times of high water, it doesn't usually take long to wake the interests of any chub in the pool, but by 4 p.m. neither of us had anything to show for our efforts. We decided that we would wait it out until dark as it seemed that our only chance might come when the light started to drop and a few chub might start to drift up into the pool.

I was almost drifting off, gazing sleepily past my quivertip at the undergrowth on the far bank when I was jolted by my rod tip thumping heavily in the rest. Reeling in a bare hook, re-baiting and casting out a fresh lobworm, I was still getting over the absurd shock of the missed bite when, within seconds of the bait landing, the rod thumped over again. I was ready for the third bite, almost expecting it, and was holding the rod, yet again I missed the savage wrench.

The fourth cast was a re-enactment of the first three, the only difference being that the bite, when it came, almost took the rod from my hands. Since I'd been casting to the same spot every time I guessed I'd been landing my lobworms in the middle of a small shoal of chub, fish which were intent on taking anything in their path. On the fifth cast I put on a huge pink prawn together with a monster lobworm, and feathered it directly over the same spot yet again, thirty-five yards out. For five minutes I sat holding the rod, at every second expecting the familiar thump, but it was only as I was placing the rod back in the rest that I felt a sharp tug. As I struck the rod hauled over. I scrambled to my feet in a desperate attempt to loosen the clutch and had just managed it before the rod pulled over until it lay level with the pool surface. Line screamed off the reel as the fish headed on an irresistible run up against the current towards the sill of the weir. Vince, seeing that I was most definitely into one of the weir pool's heavy chub, realised he was going to be needed after all, and with his bad knee hobbled over in my direction, picking up the little net on the way. Having persuaded the fish not to carry its flight into the weir sill, it was all I could do to counter other seemingly impossible runs at such a distance, out in the middle of the pool on a long line.

For another five minutes the fish rejected all my efforts to bring it across the pool, and when I gained even a little line it continued to stay deep, hugging the bottom. After what seemed like an age the line began to cut through the drifting surface suds in the current while I thought how weird this whole thing was. Weir pool chub, even the really big ones, normally show their dorsal fins or tails on the surface at some point before powering off again, but this fish, even on its long runs, hadn't left the bottom. Although the runs became shorter, they were no less frantic than when I'd hooked the fish several minutes previously.

By this time I was leaning against the trunk of the large willow just to my right, being careful that the rod tip didn't get caught in the lower branches, while the fish thudded, still unseen, just in front of us. Vince had now moved round in front of me to my left, though it didn't settle my nerves at all that he persisted in his fly swatting antics with the net, which by now was beginning to look about as small as a postage stamp. Clambering over the willow roots yet again, I missed seeing the fish roll for the first time. Vince's head was in the way. Yet just before the fish dragged the rod over on its way down to the bottom (it actually seemed to vanish into Vince's right ear), I'd had time to notice an oblique black line. I blinked, and then both Vince and I gasped as the fish finally rose in the water and lay just off the waiting net.

It was the most outlandishly huge perch either of us had ever seen. I blinked again, not wanting to see the hook pull out at the last moment. Swimming perfectly upright, the perch swam straight into the net and then lay upside down in the mesh as Vince swung it round. All we could initially see was the underside of the fish. Even from such an uncertain glimpse, Vince remarked, 'Well, that's gotta go four…'

And so it did. It measured eighteen inches and weighed an incredible 4lb 4oz. It was the most wonderful fish in the history of the world. It was a special moment for both of us, letting us both relive the day so many years ago when I netted Vince's equally fabulous perch from the little pit next to Aqueduct Lock.

As I slipped that magnificent fish back I realised it was in fact I who had been caught. To any onlooker my absorption with perch may seem like an obsession, and I myself find mere words inadequate to explain why almost every waking moment I dream of holding, just for a minute or so, another perch like it. As I watched it return to the water, and as the afternoon resumed its peacefulness, I quietly knew that for a few fleeting moments more, sometime in the future, sooner or later, I'd have to hold another.

It wasn't until I began to try and understand the character of the perch in each different water I was fishing that I started to realise what a complex creature it is. For example, what I noted as true of perch behaviour on one particular river might not be true of perch lying in a different river running perhaps only a few hundred yards away. This variability – almost, this caprice – had me raising my hat time and again to an adversary well deserving of my efforts.

In hindsight, the largest piece of the Perch Enigma Jigsaw was comprised of those moments I'd actually sat through, about fifteen minutes before I hit the fifth bite – the bite that heralded that majestic fish from King's Weir. Over the remainder of that season, and the autumn of the following two seasons, I gave liberally of my time at the weir, constantly fishing the pool for its perch and slowly adding little pieces to the puzzle.

I discovered that by far the most important thing about perch and their habits were the short periods of angling opportunity which I came to call

windows. These are bursts of intense activity by the perch, periods lasting twenty minutes or so, and over the duration of the day's fishing they may occur, if they occur at all, once or twice – with sometimes a really hectic show about an hour before dusk. On some days they may not happen at all. On others there may be only one window, just before dark, and maybe, on a really dour day, you might be lucky to experience only a five minute window which can occur at any time, depending merely on the mood of the perch on that day. In that last circumstance there's no rhyme, no reason – only the perch know.

I came to realise that my best chances were to fish as intently as I could during these windows of activity, and not waste a moment unnecessarily. During these times, a group of perch can abandon all caution and, for a short while, behave with total aggression towards anything that enters the water around them. Their aggression on these occasions almost beggars belief. On the day of the King's Weir leviathan, for instance, I'm absolutely convinced that as I cast my lobworms and prawn to a small shoal of chub which had quietly glided up into the pool, I dropped them right on the noses of one, or perhaps two, large perch which were hell bent on attacking anything that landed in front of them. In the minutes and hours before and after that little episode you would have been forgiven for thinking there wasn't a perch in the pool.

King's Weir had me in its grip and would not let me go. Time and again I returned, but whereas I'd once fished with its huge chub in mind, now my sights were set on the perch. I was used to searching the pool for bites, constantly moving the bait around until I found pockets of chub, but if I suspected perch were responsible for twitches on the quivertip and plucks on the line, I'd purposely move the bait further to elicit a response. I found that moving a bait quickly in this way would frequently provoke a half-interested perch into a decisive grab. I learned that when the perch in a particular area of a pool are going through one of their periods of intense activity then the takes defy description. I'm absolutely convinced that during these windows, the essential thing for the angler to do, is to provide a quick, sharp sudden movement to the bait or lure. After all, when a perch is in its intense feeding mode, its prey would be fleeing in blind panic, so it will naturally expect its food source to be moving quickly and trying to escape. A bait that is sitting perfectly still will only arouse mild curiosity, and at best maybe a couple of half-hearted plucks. I found that my largest King's Weir perch always came during these short bursts of activity, and after frequent casting in the same area. My mind drifts back to two days in particular – two days in the same week. It was a week when, as they say, it All Came Together – and then All Fell to Bits…

I hadn't been feeling well during the night. The previous day I'd been over to visit Keith Linsell, who in my opinion is one of the world's greatest illustrators of fish and their habitats. Since I first became aware of his art (way back when I was fifteen) it had always been one of my highest ambitions to meet him. This I most certainly did, and spent the whole day admiring his work. I was humbled to learn that he held me in the same esteem for my bird art, and although we only live about an hour's drive from each other, we'd never actually met. It was also nice to discover that Keith, in his younger days, used to fish all around the area – King's Weir included. At that time the area was also frequently fished by two other angling greats: Dennis Gander and Jack Hilton. Jack is sadly now no longer with us, but Dennis still fishes and is a very great friend of mine. He's a frequent visitor to the weir with me as we go after its perch and chub.

Such was the importance of my visit to see Keith that my nerves had been on edge all the previous day, and I hadn't managed to get any sleep, either the night before or the night after. When my feet crunched onto the gravel on The Beach my heart really wasn't really in it. I stared dully at the pool; its level was painfully low and the water ran slow and clear, the only appreciable current being in the main drag below the weir's sill. I felt the pool was almost sympathising with my sluggishness.

It wasn't long before a few tiny perch came to say hello, along with a couple of small pike which thankfully fell off as they were being played in. A lovely take out in the middle of the pool yielded a lovely perch of 2lb 2oz, and that cheered me up. Yet it was then that a series of events happened which, taken cumulatively, left me unglued.

A longish cast out into a crescent of streamer weed. Something was obviously taking an interest: the familiar jabbing on the tip, then… nothing. A few turns of the reel handle were followed by a couple more jabs… Then I felt the bait pull into some weed. Cursing, I pulled gently to free it, but it must have only provoked the fish to grab the bait. It took savagely. I struck and the rod pulled round. The fish was played in a shallow area of the pool. Then, because the fish wanted more depth, the water churned into a deep furrow. The rod tip kept on thudding heavily. I knew perfectly well that what I'd hooked was a perch. Several times it boiled heavily – big, chunky, circular boils – and I could see glimpses of a short fat shape as it curved back down to the bottom. As it neared, I could see huge dark stripes and that characteristic, hog-like back. The fish made a last heavy turn and then came to the net. It weighed 3lb exactly.

The perch was photographed and lovingly returned. I made a fresh cast, propped the rod in the rest, took two paces back… and the rod tip savagely jarred over again. The bait had obviously been taken on the drop, and the rod tip was still curved over as I pulled into yet another large perch. This one weighed 2lb 6oz.

More photos, fresh cast, same spot, bail arm over, bait settled… then the rod tip lurched over as if a couple of fighting mallards had gone through the line. There was no need to strike. The rod slammed over and stayed over, thudding solidly four or five times as I leant into the take. There was a tremendous boil about thirty-five yards out in the pool and then the fish bore down, away into deeper water. I scrambled off my chair to gain as much height as I could, and started winding down on the fish, trying to turn it and bring it back towards me. Just as I'd brought it a couple of yards in the right direction, the hook pulled. That perch felt substantially larger than the three-pounder I'd caught only minutes beforehand. Frantically, I put out another bait, thinking another big perch might be out there – but got locked into a pike, whose play was totally different from that of those big perch.

For the next couple of hours I was entertained by two more perch of 1lb 6oz each, then a couple of smaller ones, two small pike and a few missed bites. I packed up earlier than I should have done, even though the perch were most definitely on the prowl. I'd quite simply had my fill.

Over the past twenty years, losing fish hasn't really got to me as it used to. However, the hook pulling and the line falling slack on that last gigantic perch opened up all kinds of unwanted feelings that just wouldn't go away. I think that because I so wanted to see and hold another large perch as much as I did, it was all the more painful when I knew how very close I'd come. That perch really was the fish of a lifetime – and it was gone. I knew it was another four-pounder… it just had to be another four-pounder.

My quest to catch perch was now becoming an obsession. Strangely, too, it was almost as if I were afraid to hook another large perch for fear of that dreadful moment when the line fell slack again. I knew though, that before that could even happen, I would have to make the angler/perch connection first, and eager as ever, on the following trip I was at the pool a full hour before Scott and Barry – though all I had to show for my eagerness when they arrived was a thorough soaking from an early morning downpour.

Pleasantries shared and dispensed with, Scott sat to the left of me in The Beach for half an hour, then opted to go and fish No.1 East, the sill swim, which was looking superb. Barry fished all day in between us, in No.2 East. After Scott had left for No.1 East, it wasn't too long before I made a longish cast over into his side of the swim, a spot where I'd caught several large perch before in a crescent of streamer weed. This was also the same spot at which I'd lost that huge perch on my last trip.

The bait landed. I settled the rod in the rest, placed my finger over the line and sat back to watch the tip, the line as usual running freely through a V-shaped rod-rest head. The tip hadn't settled for more than a few seconds when with no preliminary twitches, no warning whatsoever, the tip pulled over decisively. I struck immediately and the rod took on a complete curve, locking solidly into a heavy fish thumping thirty-five yards away, two-thirds of the way across the pool. The water churned heavily, as always with big perch, then there was a massive boil as the fish powered to the bottom, away to my right. Then it made a long run, very fast, and doubled back before screaming off downstream.

I began to panic, not knowing whether to play the fish by back-winding or off the clutch. I was fumbling about like an old woman, stumbling this way and that, praying the fish wouldn't come off. Barry ran over, grabbed the net and asked a few pertinent questions, none of which I can now remember. This perch took line, then more line, then no line. No, the line was all over the place. No, the perch was there, still plugging away, thump, thump, thump on the rod, then a few more hauls from me to bring the fish closer, and then…

Not again.

I reeled in, inspected that useless, limp piece of line, with everything still on it: lead, link, swivels, all the bits and pieces you tie on, hook, customary bit of weed… nothing else. The four-pound perch was still out there in the pool. He probably had a sore lip, but would equally probably be back with his mates in a few minutes, with nothing more than a scuff to his bristly fins. And there was I, with another wretched memory of a lifetime.

My next cast produced a nice perch of 1lb 8oz which I took to show Scott, who had himself just landed one of 2lb 3oz, so it was obvious that the perch were really showing well. Later in the afternoon I cast out and was looking across the pool. My eyes focused idly on a relatively small patch of water lying on the far side of a curl of faster current. The spot defined itself – for no apparent reason I found myself winding in so that I could re-cast into the middle of this slack area. I remember surprising myself that I actually hit it spot-on.

Here's where it gets difficult to write, because I know what's coming next. It was the usual thing: bait lands, bail arm over, rod in the rest, finger over the line, sit back… a few seconds while everything settles, then the rod tip crawls over as if an invisible cormorant has landed on it. I'm on my feet, striking into a solid wall of fish, winding down, all in one movement, the fish heaving up to the surface in the all familiar churn… only this time, it's frightening. I'm shaking. I know it's a perch – a huge, improbably huge, perch. The boil is still spreading away, inches high, with white foam swirling in all directions. I can't loosen the clutch in time and the rod tip slams down savagely. Fumbling fingers loosen the front of the spool and off the line goes, singing under pressure and cutting across the pool. Tightening the clutch again I need to calm myself. I can't play this fish on a loose setting with line screaming all over the place… I begin to settle down into what is a mere panic. Barry's on his way over. I've settled the clutch perfectly now but this absolute bulldog of a perch has no intention whatsoever of coming across the pool. Several minutes have passed and I've made no headway at all.

Again and again I tried to bring him towards me but he would have none of it, deciding to head downstream into some decaying streamer weed. I knew exactly what he wanted to do, and with all the strain I was putting on him I was amazed that he was still able to do it. Into the weed he went and all went solid. How could I have let him get in there, when a few seconds ago he was on a free line? I didn't want to loosen right off, as I knew that to do so would give him the slack line he needed. All I could do was point the rod at him, hold the braid and let it cut the weed as he kicked. Two seconds it took, and he was free. I could feel the mush give and the perch was mine again, with the rod tip raised and the fish heavily plugging away… back into more weed. Solid again. I can't take this. Same again. Immediately the braid cuts through the weed, then a few more lunges as the rod tip is raised, and thankfully, thankfully he's still on… please, please come in… Christ, this is one hell of a p…

I reel in.

That same useless bit of line, that line with all the bits still on it, only this time with streamer weed hanging all around the hook, folded round the bend. In it comes, with those stupid little ripples coming out from it as you swing it in, silly and dripping and with the hook spinning round. Only this time the hook didn't spin round because of all the weed on it.

Barry tried to help, in a no-help-at-all kind of way. He asked me how big I thought it was. I think I replied that if there were five-pound perch in King's Weir, then that was one of them. And it was still in there – just over there, about thirty yards away. Probably with the other lost one: two gigantic fish comparing scuffs.

PIXIE DUST

Perhaps it was inevitable that the path I now found myself walking had, in a convoluted way, been quietly mapping itself out without me knowing since I was eleven or twelve years old. Every year since I was born, Mum, Dad and I spent our summer holidays in Bologna, with Mum's side of the family. Mum and I always stayed there six weeks and Dad joined us for the last two. Bologna has always been my second home, and the northern Italian way of life comes as naturally to me as life here in England. My love of birds had been instilled earlier than fishing, and Dad was already taking me to all the old fishing tackle shops around Bologna, so I could look at the stuffed birds with which they decorated their window displays.

One particular shop, situated round the back of the old part of the centre of the city, near the busy market, had in its shop front a little combination split cane rod in its own wooden case, along with a spool of line, a few cheap flies, floats and hooks and some assorted spoons. Year after year we'd return to see what new stuffed birds would be in the window, but I'd be strangely drawn to this lovely, delicate rod, which I secretly coveted. Of course, by this time, when the embers of my passion for fishing were flickering nicely, I'd already acquired a five-foot glass spinning rod and Dad had bought me the exquisite Mitchell 314 from another fishing shop not far from my Nonna's house in Via Begatto. I only mention this because these little coincidences keep cropping up all along the way in my life: *Begatto*, translated into English, is 'maggot'.

After all the years I'd been going back with Dad to see the little rod, and finally having decided I'd buy it with the money I'd saved – of course it had gone. It seemed that my window, the window opening onto the magical world of split cane, had been closed. Looking back maybe forty years, it seems strange to think it took all this time for the window to re-open, but the image of that little rod has stayed with me all my life, and the desire for it has not diminished in the slightest.

The one constant in my fishing life has always been the desire to use the lightest and most delicate of rods and tackle, and when carbon fibre came into being I switched over to it from hollow glass. When I wasn't fishing with my beloved Mitchells, I'd use all manner of centre pins for fishing close in, particularly for roach, crucians, barbel and tench. My love for fishing with these reels developed early, and over the years I'd bought several, enough to cover most fishing situations.

It was around 2002 that the angling path I'd happily been walking all those years took a sudden turn. From the moment I slooshed out of the little brook in my red plastic wellies after losing the monster dace on the rim of the minnow net, my path has been a nice comfortable amble, happily in tune with the changing moods and whims of Vince and Scott and with no revelations or surprises. For years, my little red wagon of happiness trundled on until slowly, very slowly, little bits started to fall off it. For no reason that I was aware of at first, little niggles started to creep in, and for the first time I began to look over my shoulder. The niggles certainly weren't being caused through lack of fish; I was catching just as many as I ever had, probably more. No, it was something else. First, one wheel came off, quickly followed by another. I creaked on for a while, maybe a year or so, and then when I finally realised what it was, inevitably the last two remaining wheels fell off, and in grand style. The memory of that little split cane rod was calling, mewling at me like a sad puppy, and looking over my shoulder one last time there was nothing I could do but go and pick it up.

I should have known. Reaching back into this magical world of the past was to unlock all manner of riches, far beyond anything I could have imagined at the time. I was nine again, dipping into a box of fireworks, eyes as big as sovereign pieces. Ancient cane rods, old centrepins, thread-line reels and teardrop ash and cane handled landing nets; old fishing books, traditional cork and quill floats, wicker creels… in fact everything and anything which gave me a link to an angling past that I felt I'd maybe missed out on. In my mind no time had passed at all, but now every time I go fishing I feel as if I'm stepping back through the mists and maybe sharing memories with angling friends of years gone by – friends I've never met on the bank but have encountered through reading their words, written long ago: H.T. Sheringham, 'BB,' J.W. Martin ('The Trent Otter'), and a host of others. Watching an old float lying beside the lilies, and sitting idly by an ancient, hand-crafted cane rod and thread-line reel, I can imagine dear old A.R. Matthews, the editor of *The Angler's News* himself, sitting beside me and telling me maybe to lift the float up a couple of inches or move the shot back slightly. And if I catch a nice perch or tench I quietly smile to myself, and like to think that Mr. Matthews would be smiling too. Perhaps, in truth, I'd chosen that swim through reading one of the accounts of a day's fishing he'd had himself in the early 1900s, for he too fished all around the area near St Margarets, Ware and Hertford.

Little did I know it, but this search for old items of fishing tackle would put me on many a varied trail which would lead me to befriend several new

wonderful and wonderfully charming characters who have remained my closest friends. They're all delightfully eccentric in their own way: for them, as for me, and apparently by merely dipping into this marvellous world of the past, magical things began to happen. Not only were the reels a delight to use, but the old rods had, it seems, been bestowed with pixie dust.

The first inkling that the past was welcoming me back was when I began to make enquiries into a fabulous centrepin that I'd read about in various articles in magazines and on the Internet. It was 2002, and the creator of this work of art, The Witcher Aerial, was Paul Witcher, who was then marketing the reel in co-production with his close friend Jason Inskip, a copywriter, PR guy and, among other things, a very gifted fishing writer. It was he who suggested I go and meet the pair of them for a day's grayling fishing at Nursling Weir on the River Test, so that I could see the fabled reel in action. Since I had no wish to keep all this good fortune to myself, Scott and Dave came with me, and the three of us tried for our first grayling while I looked at the fabulous reel. On a day which saw the river breaking into the fields and coursing through the meadows like watered gravy, I think the three little grayling we caught must have thought leaving the water for a couple of minutes was a better alternative to staying in it.

It was an unforgettable day though, memorable not only for the weather but also because I'd made friends with two howlingly good characters who have resisted all attempts to rain me off ever since. As the day wore on, I felt myself gravitating towards Jason's lovely old cane rod, to their Witcher Aerials, and their traditional ash and cane teardrop landing nets. If I was being drawn in then, by the time we sat drying off around an old oak table in the warm pub at the end of the day, I was truly smitten. Paul handed me the 4-inch Witcher Aerial and the prototype of a new reel he intended to make, The Longford, slightly smaller at 3½″ inches in diameter.

At some points in my life, though very rarely, I find myself speechless. In my head there are a million words, banging around like a load of captive bees in a big jar to which you'd just given a good shaking, but nothing comes out. It was like that when I saw the reels. I think a few totally inadequate attempts at speech may have escaped but as I sat in dazed silence, I seriously think I almost began to cry. Even now, as I write, words will not begin to describe these pieces of metal that Paul had somehow made animate – breathed life into by engineering. I placed my order there and then for one of each: a Witcher Aerial, and a Longford.

Sadly for me, shortly after our meeting Paul's reel making path took somewhat of a divergence and my order was indefinitely put on hold. His own path, and that of Jason's, was over the next few years to meander into film making, where he would adapt his natural artistic abilities. With his unrivalled gift of adding a touch of magic to whatever he does, Paul eventually produced a stunning film of the Avon in all her moods, entitled

Four Seasons On The Hampshire Avon, released in October 2008.

Having felt I'd spent so much time missing out on my little split cane rod – the Bologna rod from long ago – I knew I couldn't go through all this again, so donning my Sherlock Holmes hat I set out to source a reel elsewhere. Fortune smiled and not long afterwards, I found myself cradling in my trembling hands the most fabulous mint-conditioned, totally unused 4-inch Witcher Aerial. While all this was going on I'd been in constant touch with Jason and Paul by e-mail and on the phone. Because Jason lived in Hampshire and Paul in Wiltshire, the new facility of e-mail meant we could be easily and instantly in touch at any time of the day. Finding we shared the same peculiar sense of humour about all things in life, and particularly about fishing, from the very first day we hooked up I found my days that bit more bright and sparkly.

This period ushered in a whirlwind of classic tackle hunting. Jason and Paul generously introduced me to many of their talented friends, including Tim Watson, rod-maker supreme, from whom I acquired a most delectable 10′ 6″ Milward's Floatcraft which he'd personally restored.

An 11 foot Sean Linsley Mk IV Avon came trundling in after I'd tinkered on eBay, then on the same auction site I took a knock back by being outbid by a couple of pounds by a mystery bidder on a rather exquisite Bernard

Venables ash teardrop landing net top which I'd set my heart on.

I'd also made contact with a traditional float maker of extraordinary repute, Mark Price of Bristol, who began to make me exquisite, personalised floats from natural materials. Through Mark, I made friends with his delightful brother Leo, himself another aficionado of cane and pin, who in passing, happened to mentioned he knew of the mysterious bidder who'd dealt me the tragic blow during the 'Venables Net Scandal.' But his lips were sealed.

Another person I unearthed, someone who like all the others has since become a very dear friend, was Paul Cook, incredible angling artist, glass engraver, rod craftsman, float-maker – in fact all-round wizard with anything he turned his hand to. And of course, a day's fishing just isn't complete without a Paul Cook float. What's more, it seemed he also knew the identity of the fiend who'd whisked away my desired Venables landing net top like a Masked Avenger. But he wasn't saying either.

I bought several antique rods from old friend and rod guru Dennis Gander, including a couple he'd personally restored.

The heady mix of Traditional Angling Stew was being stirred, and stirred again, until all before me was a swirling cauldron of wonderment. All that was needed now was a pinch of spice – and perhaps a little touch of magic.

But just who was The Mystery Bidder, The Keeper of Bernard Venables Landing Net Tops?

The little bit of magic that was to reveal this mystery man happened in a most coincidental way, and resulted in one of the newest but best fishing friendships I've ever made. Leo, Mark Price's brother, had gone fishing for a few days with a friend of his named Gary Cullum, and sent me a disk containing photos of the pair of them. So lovely were the photos that I sent copies to another friend but quickly realised afterwards I should have sought permission first. On phoning Leo's friend Gary to apologise for my mistake and asking for belated permissions, within minutes it became obvious I was talking to a like-minded a chub, barbel, tench, carp and perch-struck individual as myself. And to one who let slip that he was the proud owner of a perfect Bernard Venables ash teardrop landing net top, which he had recently bought on eBay. The penny dropped, I was in polite conversation with none other than The Mystery Bidder, my Nemesis of the Landing Net, and… I was enjoying it immensely.

I'm sure there must be some wonderfully deep philosophical Chinese proverb that covers the eventuality of such an instant friendship being born between two completely half-eaten-biscuit lunatics. It had happened with Jason and Paul, and incredibly it had happened again with Gary Cullum, (alias 'Gobby', a nickname bestowed on him by friends because of his fondness for gudgeon). It had taken this character forty-nine years to cross my path, and now we are wasting no more time in making up for it, although the process will eventually cost him one landing net top.

To return to the fishing rods. I honestly think Tim Watson was harbouring serious doubts at his judgement in having passed his beautifully renovated Floatcraft over to me, as I began to feed back to him long lists of fish that that I began to catch with it. I really do think that this fifty-year-old rod must have been a seine net in a previous life – either that or Tim had spliced in a section of Sooty's magic wand without anyone knowing.

It was almost an embarrassment, the numbers and quality of fish that seemed to be endlessly coming to visit me on my trips, especially under the willow in a little swim Scott, another old fishing mate, Andy, and I used to fish on the River Lea in Hertford, next to the corner of the football grounds.

If the numbers of fish were an embarrassment, so too was the amount of assorted rubbish we raked out of that shallow swim over a couple of years. Being so close to the football grounds, I suppose it was inevitable that irritated types at some point or other decided to nullify their team's loss by dumping anything near to hand into the river. Given the amount of stuff we pulled out, it was extraordinary that any of us landed anything from that little stream without getting snagged up. Four office chairs, a bike frame, a couple of bike wheels, various parts of a washing machine, some rolled-up carpet, metal sheets, plastic sheets, a pair of ladies' tights (presumably from the washing machine, and I admit I actually caught these while fishing), some carpet underlay, any amount of branches, twigs and streamer weed…

We removed it all, but there was still one heavy piece of metal which I once managed to drag to the side of the bank but which gurgled back down in plumes of silt and is still there to this very day. And all this from what is a tiny, meandering stream a few yards wide, and which, above the waterline at least, looks the most perfect setting in which to fish.

I'd normally marry the Floatcraft with a delightful little 3½″ Branta, 2.5lb line and size 16 hook, and fish for roach. I'd fish the bait slightly over depth, laying-on in about four feet of water just out from the rod tip, with a Betalight in the top of the float. My tackle comprised nothing more than that. The minnows would cease activity at dusk, then the larger fish would move in. They were lovely roach of between a pound and a pound-and-three-quarters in the main, with two very notable fish of 2lb 1oz and 2lb 8oz coming to the net. Bream, too, would often show up – fish to around five pounds – and almost unbelievably, in this same swim I couldn't stop catching barbel. These were fabulous fish, the biggest weighed in at 8lb 8oz, and I quite literally lost count of the ones I caught on what was light roach tackle (ridiculously light for barbel).

To top everything, I even landed a mirror carp of twelve pounds on the same evening as two of the largest barbel. Time and time again the float would slide off into the darkness, and I'd be locked in a twenty minute tussle amongst overhanging trees and acres of dense streamer weed with the fish charging off thirty yards downstream and then up again, through sunken branches and bulrushes and all the aforementioned snags, only for the rod to win through…

No, Tim, you can't have that Floatcraft back.

While all this was going on I'd also been showing the 11′ Sean Linsley Avon that I had bought on eBay, to all manner of carp at our club lake in Nazeing. It's steeped in history, this lake – one of two situated either side of a narrow dividing path off Green Lane. The lakes used to be a favourite haunt of great fishing buddies Jack Hilton and my good friend and mentor, Dennis Gander. It was at this time, the late 1960s, that the fishing artist Keith Linsell was also casting his line here. During this period, Nazeing was going through a phenomenal phase of big perch captures and, obviously, this species had all these illustrious names by the throat – just as it had me.

Back to the present. I'd discovered that two big perch had been caught by accident at Nazeing, and I'd also noticed a great deal of surface fry feeding going on, so I was giving a couple of lovely old cane rods an airing and was free-lining some lobworms in a swim among the trees I rather fancied on the west bank.

After a couple of hours with nothing but a half-hearted lift on an indicator and a lost carp to keep me company, I got the fidgets – as I normally do. I kept looking at the Linsley Avon in the rod bag and decided to get it out. Idly, I put on Paul's Witcher Aerial, ran a tiny porcupine quill three feet up the line, tied on a strong size 4 hook and wrapped a piece of flake around it. I reeled in the two rods which I had been fishing, picked up my sublime cane Barder Venables landing net (one I'd acquired from Jason and which Gary had obviously missed), and ambled along the deserted bank, stifling a yawn.

I stopped at the corner of the lake in a jungle of overhanging willows, trunks, branches and snags, and unhitched the hook and flake from the cork handle. Placing the landing net at my feet and wondering quite what the hell I was doing all this for – after all, I was supposed to be perch fishing – I lightly swung out the flake a few feet in front of me so that it landed in a small gap among the snags. Yawning again, blinking, I watched the flake slowly sink out of sight. I suppose it had only drifted down a foot before I lost sight of it.

Then I noticed the tiny porcupine quill zip forward an inch. I struck, and as my rod tip clawed vertically down to the surface of the water, something as surprised as myself began to rise up in the water. Jolted into full consciousness, I instinctively reeled down and heaved up in one and the same movement. There was a churning water vortex as a massive fish tried to gain momentum, but I knew that to allow this to happen was to lose all, so I used the elasticity of the rod to roll the fish over and over on a short line while reaching for the net and then extending it. Within twenty seconds I had the net out to the fish and on its next roll, the one which I sensed would have had it sounding to the bottom and off to who knows where, the fish just turned over and dived straight into the mesh.

It was that easy.

I cut the line and carefully carried the fish back to my swim where I rested, weighed it and got someone to come and take some photographs. It was an absolutely immaculate mirror carp. The scales finally decided to give up trying at 31lb 6oz. As it registered the weight, my mind drifted back to Bob Richards on that day of days – October 3rd, 1951, on the banks of Bernithan Pool – when he landed the then record carp, also a mirror, of 31lb 4oz.

Super Landing Net Man, Gary Cullum, a.k.a. Gobby, comes in a bundle of guises, but because of a spelling error in signing off in one of his twenty million e-mails to me, he is now known to me as 'Goob.'

Somewhere along the way, during our desire for catching up on lost time, I happened to mention to Goob that I was on the look out for one of the most desirable of desirable cane rods, the Allcock's Lucky Strike. Dennis had been restoring one, and I'd been eyeing it up on many visits to his house, and I'd reached the point of standing in Charlie Bucket's shoes at the Wonka Factory Gates on this one. If the subsequent events read almost like a fairy story, then it's because it is, with the most remarkable ending.

Christmas Eve, 2007. Once upon a time, not so very long ago, I got a phone call. It was Goob.

'Mole, I'm coming over your way, can't stop, but I'll be at Simpson's just off the M25 in half an hour. Got to give something to you.'

(I knew what it was, so...) 'Okay mate, I'll give you the money.'

'You haven't seen it yet. I don't want any money at the moment – you might not like it. Try it first. Have a fish with it. Use it, break it, then we'll sort it out later.'

'No,' I said, 'I won't have it any other way. I have to give you the money.

I know I'll love whatever it is.'

'Yeah, yeah, we'll sort it out. See you in half an hour.' (Click.)

I met Goob at the pre-arranged spot; it was raining and he was in his car. He opened the door and before I could hand over anything, a small rod-tube with an envelope wrapped round it was shoved into my hand.

'Gotta go. Gotta drive half way round the M25 and pick up a load of honey. See ya…' With that he was gone. Christmas Eve, and I was left there standing in the rain beside my car with a rod tube in my hand.

On returning home I opened the tube. I was five again, in a world of red buses and fire engines. The little rod sparkled and twinkled while I could feel the natural life of the cane warming up along my arm.

Then I noticed the letter. – it had a wax seal on the back. On the front it said 'phone Goob before opening'. Reluctant to put the rod down, awkwardly, with my left hand, I phoned Winnie the Pooh, who was still on the M25, on the way to his beloved honey pots. He insisted this dream of a little rod, lovingly restored by Gary Marshall, was to be paid for by a kind of Royal Consent, and only when I'd been clever, or lucky enough, to catch a perch weighing 2lb 10oz with it. Then, and only then, could I open the letter and discover the full amount that I owed. There had been brief mentions in various cryptic e-mails of £5 per ounce, so even with my appalling grasp of mathematics, it was working out in the region of £210. As this went against the natural way I did things, I just had to get out and catch a perch of 2lb 10oz on the rod as quickly as I possibly could. Then I could safely feel that the rod was truly mine – and I would have paid for it.

Because a debt had to be paid, a fish had to be caught…

The first opportunity I had was to join Andy in our little perch corner on the Rib in Hertford. It was a classic Mr. Crabtree swim on a very tight sweeping bend. All the perch hold up under the branches of old, dead bushes which hug the other side. Andy and I sat opposite the perch-hold, on the inside of the bend, high up on a grassy bank, hidden amongst dead and dying vegetation. As usual in this swim we sat together with me on the left, the upstream side, with Andy quiver-tipping lobworms from the downstream end. Although we fished in entirely different ways, we managed to hold our baits within feet of each other. I inched a yellow-tipped float along the edge with a lobworm just nudging bottom. Of course, I was on a mission to catch a perch of 2lb 10oz.

Fish after fish hit the landing nets, with Andy catching perch of 1lb 5oz, 1lb 11oz, 2lb, 2lb 8oz, plus a chub of 2lb 9oz. I managed chub of 6oz, 10oz, 1lb, 2lb 12oz, and perch of 1lb, 1lb 2oz, 1lb 4oz, 1lb 9oz, 2lb 5oz, and (tantalisingly) 2lb 6oz. Although pixie dust was indeed twinkling down on the pair of us, I couldn't eke out those extra few ounces.

It finally happened a few days later on December 31st, when I fished the same swim with Vince. I had two bites. One was a two-pound pike and the other was a beautiful perch which, after a lot of deliberation and weighing on three sets of scales, averaged out at exactly 2lb 10z. I was elated. At last I could settle my debt, and it was with a light heart that I returned home that evening to open the sealed letter at long last, cheque book at the ready...

Christmas Eve 2007

To my dear friend Mole,

Yellow and black-trimmed Gold Label Lucky Strike. You catch a 2.10 perch before we discuss – that I will tell you verbally today, Christmas Evening 2007. When you catch your 2.10, to be weighed and witnessed, even if by yourself, then the rod is yours, a gift from Goob. Until then it is on loan and only loan. I hope you have enjoyed its bend, its curve and its sweetness.

And Hooray, for now, on opening this letter, you have used the little L.S. to catch your 2.10. Well done you. Every man, nay, every fisher forever the boy, should have a Lucky Strike. Today you earned that rod. It is yours to cherish. I hope it gives you many more years of pleasure, though that depends on what the date is today when you are reading this note. I hope you are not old and grey, for surely no perch fisher waits so long for his desired fish! Perhaps he does – You are, Sir, a friend indeed, and now deserving owner of my Lucky Strike.

I remain, as ever,
Gary

THE LIST SO FAR

Looking back to the first time I met Dennis Gander, I can admire the patience he must have shown at the inane comment I passed on the antique tackle he was using ('You must be angling for old fish, ha ha'). He must have forgiven my idle remark, for it wasn't until we'd bounced into each other a couple more times that I began to realise how slow on the uptake I'd been, and I became enlightened to just who Dennis Gander was. I've now come to know him very well and having spent numerous, extremely fulfilling evenings in his company, chatting into the small hours about all manner of things. I feel intoxicated by his love for life and the appreciation of all the good things in it: fishing, of course, and traditional photography and a kaleidoscope of other subjects. I normally have to drag myself out of his house at some insane hour, only to return home and not be able to sleep, thanks to my mind still reeling at his stories.

In his fishing life, Dennis has done just about everything you could ever imagine, times ten. Then multiply that again by another ten… and again. He's been at the forefront of much of what we see today regarding rod design, tackle, accepted angling methods and practices. He and his close circle of friends probably devised them – Walker, Stone, Taylor, Hilton, all fished with and conversed with Dennis. And on every subject regarding fishing – and if a problem presented itself, Dennis's incredibly inventive mind was invariably in the middle sorting things out. Many tackle ideas now attributed to others were in reality derived from seeds first sown by Dennis.

If you could ever draw up some endless list of the items of tackle we all use today, together with a further list of the accepted ways of catching fish, at some point, and usually at the conception stage, all these lists are roads which lead to Rome – or rather, to Dennis. I honestly think you could pick nearly any item of tackle at random, and somewhere in its history, Dennis' name would crop up.

His life in tournament casting is another story. For a period of several years he was on fire in the tournament casting world, setting a national record and achieving world and UK firsts. I love his stories from his past, not only of fishing with legendary anglers, but of the days when he was an avid collector of things as diverse as antique fishing tackle or tin toys or even vintage Leica cameras. Any time spent in the company of this man, whether at home with his lovely wife Edie, or on the banks fishing, is to be truly savoured.

This all brings me, albeit in a rather chaotic, jumbled fashion, to the List So Far, which I take pride in having invented myself and which within my small special circle of friends, has quietly become some kind of dubious institution. However…

Because of the ease with which we can all stay in touch with one another using e-mail, I set up this List So Far. It's run for a number of years and is still happily trundling as I write. Effectively, on any given fishing trip, should any of us be fortunate enough to better the weight of a fish which heads the list in a particular category, then that fish topples the one of the previous captor. Naturally this has caused much merriment between all of us – on the occasion, for example, when Paul may have caught roach locally on one of his waters which bettered one of mine from a similar water, which may have headed the list for a season or more. Over the years the weights on the List So Far have slowly increased, to a point where the list itself is quite impressive. Under three main headings of Stillwaters, Rivers and Small Streams, I've managed somehow to keep our raggedy bunch of pirates in hand and compile a list which is quite fun to look back on – especially when my name is on it.

We've even taken the List So Far one step further, using Jason's idea of the Angler's McNab: three specimen fish, of different species, on one particular day. To commemorate such captures I put up a small trophy – a little hand-carved Japanese netsuke of three carp. This is passed on to the next fortunate captor on a red-letter day when another three specimen fish of different species are caught. It goes without much saying that achieving such a McNab is a very rare occurrence. Goob then thought up the *Cullum Brace Stone,* which is a small, rounded flat stone on which I painted a tench and a roach. Anyone catching a specimen brace of fish of different species would be the new owner for a while, until the next brace was caught by someone else, at which point the *Cullum Brace Stone* would be handed over.

It's all great fun and a nice way to stay in touch, to see on a regular basis how each of us are faring in our fishing in different parts of the country. And it really isn't that strange if you think about it. It all began many years ago with a simple little split cane fishing rod in the window of an old shop in the back streets of Bologna. All it needed was a little boy to press his nose against the glass – and wish. From this wish grew a small, meandering path which he followed, and along the way he became showered with the wonderment of glittering pixie dust and wonderful, caring friends. No – it's not strange. Not strange at all.

Opposite page - clockwise from top left:
Dennis Gander; Gary Cullum a.k.a. Goob; Doug Pledger (my brother);
(group shot – left to right) Vince Cawley, Steve Tibble, Me, Scott Poyner

CHUB IN THE SHADOW OF RICHARD WALKER

As he slowly slid unnoticed into the quiet backwater of the stream, nothing was disturbed by his arrival. Using the trickle caused by the gravels on the shallows to break up his shadow as he entered the pool, he slipped alongside some thin strands of bistort and then paused, just under the trailing edge of some old willow roots. He enjoyed the warmth of the sun on his back as it burnt off the early morning mist.

The water here is clear as air and his eye takes in every movement in the pool immediately around him. Tiny water shrimps scuttle around in the silt and a dragonfly nymph grabs at a small gudgeon fry, momentarily catching it, but not quite strong enough to keep hold. His eye follows the movements of a group of snails crawling round the bistort. They hold his interest for a few seconds but minute impulses of hunger in his brain override any idle thoughts and his eye flicks back, looking for signs of something with which to satiate an empty stomach. A little group of perch dart and flicker through, harrying some unfortunate fry. These perch would in themselves, on another occasion, make an easy mouthful, but only when feeding with such abandon that all caution is forgotten, usually in the evening, just on dusk. In those instances even baby ducklings, frogs and small water voles may be blindly attacked without a moment's thought. In the long, dragging days of winter, even the little shrimps would be enough to raise some kind of interest, just for a few moments, but today it would take far more than that.

He slowly glides round a pre-determined beat, his beat, and returns to the old willow roots where once again he pauses. He rests at this same spot for several minutes at a time, then repeats his journey around the backwater. He's resting up, his fins arbitrarily curling slightly as he edges across the current now and then to allow a piece of weed to drift by.

I can sense he's at ease in his world. I've been watching him for a while now, from behind a large willow on the opposite bank. Sitting on the ground, leeward side to the stream, I lean against the old trunk and look across the fields to a Tunnicliffe painting of a group of black and white cows contentedly chewing at the grass, tails flicking. I have with me a wand-like carbon 8 foot fly rod, the 'Ribtickler' – a wisp of a rod, specially made for me, with a short, straight cork handle to accommodate a small fixed-spool reel. I suppose this desire for the tiniest, lightest of rods must hark back to that little spinning rod of Doug's. Even now, the thought of troubling that chub for a few minutes with anything more than what I deem barely necessary is abhorrent.

My reel is the usual Mitchell, this time the baby 408. It's loaded with some 4lb line, greased for the last few yards, to the end of which is knotted a size 8 hook. I'm using nothing else. My eye flicks down, chub-like, to the big can of lobworms.

There's no rush. I know where my chub will be, and if he isn't at his station by the willow roots next time I look, I know for sure he'll be there again within a few minutes, after his tour of the backwater. Getting up from the old trunk I can still feel three or four deep ridges in my back, left by the furrowed bark. Thirty-five years ago the tree would have looked and felt much the same, but being slightly more impatient and flittish then I probably would not have sat for so long had I not seen the fish. Of course today's chub wouldn't have existed then, but I have no doubt that his grandfathers, and their more distant ancestors, would have been doing just the same thing. Back then, the lie of the pool was doubtless the same; the chub lay in exactly the same place.

I'd like to think that Dick Walker sat in this very spot, took off his famous hat, maybe wiped his brow, looked back at his fish and wondered – just as I'm wondering now. How would the great man have tackled 'my' chub's great grandfather? A mist is forming. Through it I can see him with his dear friend, Pete Thomas. Perhaps they were both here, under this very tree. I'd like to think Dick would have leaned back against this old trunk and offered Pete the chance to try for 'their' chub while he lit up a cigarette and watched. Perhaps Dick was on his own, as I am today. Only the willow would know for sure.

I look up at the sun glittering through the leaves and smile, then I too open the can of lobs, just as I know Dick would have done.

Kneeling, I have a dense stand of reed sweet-grass lying between me and the water, and will need these grasses to break up any image the chub may get of me. Peering through the green blades I can make him out two inches below the surface, in the same spot by the old roots, just as I'd expected. I put his weight at a good four and a half pounds, an extremely heavy fish for a little stream such as the Rib.

For a split second the sun is blotted out, and then instantly reappears. I turn, look up.

A heron has circled over, and in passing the sun, has momentarily blackened everything out. In the same instant, a myriad of small fish, tiny fry, bursts on the surface, which in itself is enough to unsettle the chub, causing him to sink lower in the water. I must wait a few moments while he either drifts back up or the irritation sets him off on another tour of his pool.

I take the opportunity to crawl back to collect my rod and hook up a big lobworm. On returning, I peer over to see that he has come back, and by his manner I can see he is once again at ease. Keeping constant eye contact with the chub, I remember the dace long ago, in the little brook at the end of my garden. From this point onwards I won't take my eyes off him. If I detect anything that suggests he thinks something is wrong, then I'll stop and wait for him to relax. All the time I'm slowly creeping nearer, opening the bail arm and readying the rod and reel for my cast – hopefully the only one I'll need. Every movement I make, where I place my feet, any twigs and reeds I have to push aside… all these things occur in the periphery of my vision as I make my way purely by feel along the bank.

At some point I sense I must make the cast. A cast that must be the merest gentle flick of the rod tip, held low. The weight of the worm is enough in itself to cover any distance needed – usually, on a stream like the Rib, only three or four yards. I can often sense, even while the worm is in the air, whether or not the chub will take. In this respect, for perhaps one second, I like to think I have the upper hand. In that delicious blink of an eye I know, before he does, that the lobworm will land within inches of the chub's nose. It's even better if it lands just to one side of his tail since the splash of it landing will give him only two options. It will either scare him into the next pool as effectively as if I were to drive my car up to the bank, lever a plank of wood across the hooter and leave it on all day, or (I eternally hope) working out of the sublime mixture which makes the chub a chub – instinct, hunger and blind cussedness – he will cannonade the worm before he even realises he's done so.

The plop of the lobworm is drowned by a churning swirl of water. Of course, by the time I have snicked the rod tip, the chub and I are connected by a thin, taut line among a cascade of spray. Sometimes it isn't easy to persuade a chub out of his cartwheels, for unless there is deep water nearby he'll continue to be reckless in his flight on being hooked. Luckily, being a big chub, he'll usually head towards the deeper water under the roots where he'll plug away heavily. I've now moved round downstream of him, glad of his decision not to carry on his flight in a series of leaps, but to be honest I knew he wouldn't – not a chub of his weight.

The fragile little rod is in a complete arc, the 4lb line is matched perfectly; although it's very fine there's no way it can break while the rod's flexed. Feeling his body weight, his every move, I can sense every twist and turn he makes. The rod's pressure is slowing him down, even calming him as he seeks sanctuary in the darkness under the roots. Presently, after what is perhaps only a minute or two, I notice a few thin strands of streamer weed floating up from the undercut, followed by a dull brassy flank twisting deep as the chub grudgingly rises up. A chub will resign himself eventually, as he knows the refuge of the roots are behind him, unlike perch who are always indignant and thrashing wherever they are – coming to the net, in the net, or being released. You can never take your eyes off a perch when he's coming to the net because you can never know when he will thrash, and that is when most of them are lost. My chub has a few more rolls left in him, yet the softness of the rod kindly suggests to him that a last prolonged dive for the roots is best left for another day. I lean down to pick up the old cane landing net and gently drift him towards me. He comes into the mesh. I free him from the hook and rest him for a few moments inside the net at the water's edge while I prepare the camera and scales. I quickly take a few photos, weigh him, and gently return him to his pool, where he drifts off and disappears down under the roots of the willow.

The River Rib is a charming little stream. Anglers older than I delight in telling me how different it all was years before I arrived on the banks. In fact I think I did experience the back end of these golden days as I remember well the awful period when, at the behest of anonymous people in offices, the dredger was sent out and ruined the little paradise that flowed through Hertford. The dredger came and went, leaving in its wake a river which seemed to be a fish bone of what it once was. I couldn't bear to return for several years but in the end I couldn't stay away. I was delighted to find the spirit had never left the stream; she had just waited for the dredger to move on and then, once it had gone, she could return and breathe life back into the place she loved.

Although the Rib is home to many species of fish, the two which have mainly courted my interest over the years are the chub and perch. I suppose the reason for this must be attributed to the way I've decided to fish: the free-lined lobworm. Both chub and perch are opportunistic in their feeding habits, and a big lobworm dropped carefully at any point along the stream is likely to be seen by any fish that happens to be nearby. At certain times, roach and dace will turn on to a worm easily enough, and so too bream and barbel, of which there are a few scattered sporadically along its length.

I have found that roach, bream and barbel tend to show up on days of more sedentary fishing, times when the lobworm is left to sit around on the bottom for a good long while, usually under a float or on a ledger. I think that on days of high, coloured water these fish will come to net more frequently when big lobworms are used as bait. Dace are a law unto themselves and will attack a ten inch lobworm whenever they feel like it.

Isolated pockets of rainbow trout, escapees from a trout farm at West Mill, have over the years worked their way downstream through the little staggered weirs which punctuate the length of the Rib. In high water these weirs, which in effect are just drops in stream level, even out and fish can easily be swept from one section of river into the section below. On a quiet day with the chub, these rainbows can be pleasing enough to catch, but for some reason rainbow trout have never pressed any of my buttons.

Now and then a brown trout shows up. Again, as with the rainbows, brownies struggle for my affections, but one day I did see, fleetingly, a big old rogue male cruise through an inaccessible area of water only a foot deep. I think he must have weighed a good five pounds. Now that fish I could easily have lost some sleep over.

And that leaves me with pike and eels, both of which I generally love to death, yet strangely, while free-lining worms on the Rib, they interest me not one jot. And so, back to the chub.

CHUB IN THE SHADOW OF RICHARD WALKER

To me the chub has always been a more visible fish than the perch. I think he's more prone to basking or cruising the open water, just below the surface. He'll have his marked-out beat just as the brownie does: he'll work the area, then turn and swim back downstream with the current, slightly faster than the flow. On reaching the downstream end of his beat, he'll swing across and slowly work his way back up again. Sometimes he'll do this on his own, or he'll stagger it with two or three others, depending on the size of the shoal. Depending on the chosen area of residence and the size of chub in question, the numbers in the shoal will vary. In a small, narrow run there may be just a couple of medium sized fish, three at most, of around one to two pounds. Then again, some little runs seem to be home to a whole gathering of smaller fish, with none of them larger than a few ounces.

One particular spot I crept up on – a shallow cattle-drink bordering the edge of a gravel run only inches deep, alongside a sudden drop-off into a long deep pool – was obviously home to a whole squadron of big chub. On one particular hot, sunny afternoon, the cattle hadn't been down to drink, they were all lying up in the cool shade of the hawthorns elsewhere around the field. No-one had been in to feed the horses either, and I arrived at just the right time. The entire shoal of chub, or so it seemed, was holding at the base of the shallows, right over the drop-off. I guess there must have been a dozen chub in that one spot with their backs out of the water, all side by side, inches from each other.

Creeping up on the shoal was easy enough, and something I'd done many times before, even without any cover. As always with chub in this situation I knew what to expect so, as the lobworm arched over to the shoal and descended, I prepared myself for the eruption I knew would assuredly happen. In the subsequent explosion of spray I found myself attached to one of the leaping fish, but in the confusion, quite which one it was impossible to tell. At first the whole shoal leapt frantically, shadowing the twists and turns of the hooked fish in the shallow water, but in the seconds that followed they collected their senses and drifted back into the deeper water of the pool, while I guided my fish back to the net. Weighing about two pounds, I think he was about average for the shoal, but on other occasions after dark we'd taken single fish, the best being 4lb 9oz from the same spot.

By presenting a lobworm in this manner, you're robbing the chub of the chance of examining the bait, and as this is one of the main tricks in his armoury to prevent you going home happy, it's one you should always take advantage of should the occasion present itself. Because I only write from my own experience, I couldn't say if other baits would elicit the same response. I have a feeling that only a natural bait such as a worm, slug or crayfish would be set upon in this manner. Having said that, I'd include an artificial fly in this category, as the fly would represent a natural food item. Being an imitation of something natural, there would be no reason for the fish to be scared or wary of it, unless of course it was badly presented or the shoal had become unduly nervy before you had a chance to make the cast.

I remember creeping up on a large shoal of dace once with a big bushy chub fly one hot afternoon. Making a longish upstream cast, I dropped the thing smack in the middle of what must have been forty fish lying in three inches of rippling water. I think every fish in that shoal must have decided to launch itself at the fly at precisely the moment I feathered it onto the surface. Of course every one of them missed, and I think the explosion of spray unsettled them so much that the whole lot just disappeared.

Fishing the dry fly for chub presents tremendous opportunities to do all the creepy-crawly, cowboys-and-Indians, secret-agent stuff, dodging behind bushes and hiding behind trees. Sometimes I feel all this is so much fun that I really wouldn't be bothered too much if I didn't see a chub all day. In fact, during the last couple of years or so, I've taken to wearing a rather nice Man from Uncle badge on my fishing jacket, just to make things official as it were, in case any poor misinformed soul were to wonder quite what the hell I was up to.

No-one reading this should get the idea that I know anything about flyfishing. I don't. Let me just sneak a mention of it in now though, quiet as a church mouse, for my own benefit, then I can carry on. If I can pull the wool and feathers over the eyes of a few chub, that will be good enough for me, so I won't insult anyone else's intelligence by suggesting I know what I'm doing. The mere fact I can open the fly box and select a fly that looks as though it could float long enough to survive my constant attempts at bouncing it off trees before it sinks suggests my choice was the right one. Of course the fly has to run a gauntlet of windknots, endless tangles and every conceivable object within the distance of a short walk. Plus the inevitable crack-offs, magnetised reeds and bushes and who-knows-what-else, in front of me and behind, sideways, up and down. You begin to realise the wisdom of forgetting the fishing altogether, and just getting back to the business of re-living events at the OK Corral.

In my own defence though, on most days I do have the ability to sneak up close enough to a chub to pat it on the head, so the necessity of going through all the preambles of false casting and the like doesn't often come into play. Most of the time all I need do is pull off a little line and drop a

M.J.PLEDGER.

big, bushy fly right over the nose of the unsuspecting fish, just the same as I would do a lobworm. The greatest compliment a fish can pay me when I'm flyfishing is constituted by the actual moment when it rises to take the fly. It is at this instant that I get my greatest satisfaction, and it's immaterial whether the fish is a three ounce dace or a chub worthy of red letters in Izaak Walton's notebook.

It wasn't until I'd learnt to wait to strike only after a really slow count of four when flyfishing for River Rib chub that I eventually started to show some of them the inside of my landing net. Up to that point, all the dastardly creeping up on other secret agents, tailing the bad guys and sneaking round the shadows counted for nothing. I even got proficient at snaking out seemingly expert long casts, missing every snaggy branch and twig within twenty yards, placing the fly delicately within inches of undercut banks where fish were holding up, only to be beaten at the last moment because of striking too early. By waiting a good four seconds, even if the fish hadn't turned down and away with the fly, success was more or less assured. Even then most of the chub were only lightly hooked in the extreme edge of the mouth or in the scissors.

One chub, a fish I'll never forget, really did turn the tables on me. I was walking back along an impenetrable twenty-yard stretch of blackthorn bushes which were intermingled with an old rusty barbed wire fence which flanked a steep, eighteen-inch drop to the water. On the other side of the bushes and wire the water was still, about three feet deep. Through the blackness of twigs and thorns, the only pockets of water I could see were at ground level, where rabbits had nibbled the blackthorn leaves away, and worn down a few of the lower twigs. It was absolutely guaranteed that this twenty yard stretch had never seen a fishing rod in years. The rabbits said so.

Even if I'd had lobworms with me, I wouldn't have given the bushes a second glance, given the impossibility of it all. As my eye angled downwards while I negotiated cow-pats in the field, I happened to notice a tiny dimple in the water through the tangle of blackthorn where the rabbits had been. For some reason I stopped and crouched down to look through the restricted area between all the twigs – and noticed another dimple, further along, behind the bushes. I backed off into the field and looked again at the problem. I was faced with an impenetrable wall of blackthorn except for a miserable gap about a foot high lying over a load of rabbit holes. Behind all this, a chub – I was sure it was a chub – was quite happily doing the rounds of his pool, every now and then tipping up towards the surface to sip in a little insect trapped there in the film. He had grown large in his secluded pool, safe from all intruders behind the castle wall, and… my mind was wandering. To be honest, I wasn't angling for the fish, I was angling for the challenge. I just wanted to see if I could catch an 'impossible' fish.

I lay on my stomach on the outside of the barbed wire fence and laid my tiny wisp of a fly rod alongside me on the grass. The fly was already tied on, a size 16 black dry fly. I pushed the small landing net as far through the gap as I could, until the end of it was level with the water's edge. I then followed, edging forward like a lizard, dragging the rod tip alongside my nose, feeling the barbed wire and lower twigs and thorns catch in the back of my neck and jacket as I inched towards the water. Thinking back, it must have taken me ten minutes to finally crawl into a position from which I could do… absolutely nothing, other than have a nose-to-nose conversation with any rabbit daft enough to come out of his hole.

I eventually ended up by the water's edge. By my left ear was the landing net, by my right ear, the rod tip. It was all I could do to swivel my head from side to side without dragging my chin into the bank. Anyway, there I was. To be quite honest, given the extreme heat, the claustrophobic surroundings, and the fact I could hardly move cocooned as I was, I could just as easily have closed my eyes and gone to sleep. And yet while I'd been going through all this nonsense the rising fish had continued dimpling every now and then and I'd worked out the area of his beat. He passed by, maybe not two feet away from my face, but because of the angle of the light still I could not see him. As before there was just the merest ripple as he took something trapped in the surface film.

With a great deal of trouble and effort, cursing, and then apologising to rabbits for unseemly language, I managed to pull out a foot of line from the tip ring. I then had to somehow push the rod slightly further out over the water, my idea being to dangle the fly delicately on the surface and await the chub's arrival next time round. It took ages but somehow I must have managed it, because I remember finally being poised with the rod jammed under my chest, grasping it by the ferrule, and three feet of the rod top over the water with a foot of line hanging from the tip and the fly resting in the surface film.

Presently I could see the fish approaching, ten feet away. A few seconds later, in line with the fly, there was another vague movement about three feet nearer. At that moment I vibrated the rod, causing the fly to jiggle up and down as if it were a bluebottle struggling to lift off. The take was the most natural and perfect one I'd ever seen. Unhurriedly, with all the time in the world, he took the fly and within a second it was as if nothing had ever been there – no fly, no fish, just calm, undisturbed water. One-twenty, two-twenty, three… three seconds. I couldn't wait to a count of four. I gently snicked the rod tip and the chub and I were attached.

At first the fish did nothing. I don't think he'd even realised anything was amiss. I hadn't exerted any pressure on him at all after setting the hook, for the simple reason that in my cramped position there was nothing I could do. I didn't want to alert him further to anything possibly being wrong in his day, so I just fed out line as best I could, but I knew that with every passing second the drag of the fly-line would make him realise that things were not entirely as they should be. After a minute or so the inevitable point was reached: the drag built up, and he started to plug away in the deeper area of the pool. All I could do was feed line through the rings as and when he needed it, without actually moving the rod at all, hoping at some point he would tire and let himself be drawn near enough to net.

This surreal state of affairs continued for at least fifteen minutes, during which time I still hadn't seen him. Occasionally I'd see his vague form turning over and I strangely began to wish he'd throw the fly. Perhaps he really deserved to be spared the embarrassment of the net. After all, he'd risen to the fly, and hadn't I always said that such an instant was the moment of my greatest satisfaction? At the same time I felt I was now here for the ride and that I really should stick around to remove the hook for him. I began to feel sorry I'd ruined his afternoon, and wished he'd settle things by losing the fly for me. However, at long last he tired, and after several near misses I guided him safely into the net.

I should have guessed that the chub of my dreams was actually living elsewhere and was not the fish now cradled in the mesh of my landing net. Still lying on my stomach, I unhooked him and gazed on the huge form of a small stream, four-pound, rainbow trout, with a kype like that of a big old brownie. I was sure that he was an escapee from the trout farm upstream. Perhaps he'd escaped when he was but a mere tiddler, had been washed down in the floods and over the years had been left alone to grow large behind his castle wall. He was truly a magnificent fish.

I gently released him and watched him swim off back to his pool, knowing that I'd probably be the only angler ever to catch him, and that he would continue to grow on to an ever larger size. Who knows? He may even live there still today, maybe by now an old grandfather trout weighing into double figures, still living out his life in the little pool behind the blackthorn wall.

M.J.PLEDGER.

One chub which didn't turn into a trout lived with his mate at the extreme end of our fishery at West Mill, a few yards upstream of a busy road bridge. If I'm strictly truthful, those two chub were being a bit naughty because they lay a few yards out of bounds, on the other side of our boundary, and as such should really have been given a warning, but being a forgiving soul, I let them off.

They ventured out in only inches of water in a little gully about a foot wide which had been created by debris jammed amongst sticks and branches which jutted out from either bank of the narrow stream. The water here was so rippling and shallow that when they held station, at the point where the gully was at its most narrow, their backs were frequently out of the water. It was a natural position for them to lie since all manner of food drifting down on the current would obviously be drawn right over their heads. As they were the two largest chub in the area they'd taken this prime position and the smaller fish were dotted around below them – here, there and all over the place. The smaller of the two looked about four-and-a-half pounds but the big one, a dark old warrior, must have bested him by a good pound. Obviously he was the one I had my eyes on.

Owing to the nature of the stream at this particular point, fishing from the bank was impossible. The only recourse was to get into the water below the bridge and quietly wade up underneath it, out into open air again, and then to start creeping up on these two fish, which were still a good twenty yards upstream. The first time I tried, everything I did went wrong and of course, chub being chub, they put up with my ineptitude for only a couple of minutes before they disappeared. I returned the next day, and the next. No matter what I did, something would happen to mar my chances, usually a miscast or a hang up in the snags. Although I kept returning periodically, once I'd put those chub down they didn't come back. I think it was because they were so vulnerable and visible in the shallow water. Anything in the tiniest bit untoward – and even on my best day I was capable of delivering just that – and they were off.

The nearest I got was to be my last attempt, because after this little episode, I just gave up on them. As usual I found myself walking towards them under the bridge, when all of a sudden I noticed a small shoal of six chub, all about eight inches long, drift down towards me and then use my left boot to hold against in the current. I held my rod up vertically with the tip nearly touching the water, pulled out a foot of line and tried to dangle the fly at my feet. After a few minutes of this farce I began to see the absurdity of it all and continued in my quest for the two bigger fish, leaving the little shoal wondering where their snag had gone.

On that day I'd decided to tie on a special little fly my good Tasmanian mate, John Morwood, had given me. It was a clever little thing called the 'gum beetle'. Absolutely deadly out in Tasmania, it's nothing more than a small circular piece of black duplon cut from an old rod handle and tied onto a hook. Out in Tassie the gum trees which overhang the streams at certain times of the year are full of little beetles – gum beetles. These look something like big, fat, blackish ladybirds. Now and then they fall into the water with a loud plop, and the trout love them. The artificial fly, being made of duplon, cannot sink, and this is what gave me the idea to use it on this occasion.

On previous trips I'd placed a supposed dry fly perfectly over the gully, only to have fate intervene and drown the thing. I swear that on a couple of occasions the sunken dry actually even passed underneath the chub, which were naturally looking upwards for their dinner. In theory at least, the gum beetle imitation couldn't sink, and in any case chub aren't particularly choosy when it comes to flies, so anything vaguely edible floating over their heads would stand a very good chance of getting taken… providing I didn't put it up a gum tree.

The chub were there and feeding. I crept up as near as I could so I wouldn't need too much false casting. First cast saw the little gum beetle land over their heads, perfectly in line with the gully, about six feet upstream, and as the current slowly drew it back towards the fish, I could see the smaller, lighter one of the two move slightly across the current, position himself, rise and take it as it passed over his head. No waiting, no counting, I tightened up as he turned down and there was an insane boil in the gully. The chub shot off upstream, neatly circling a big stand of reeds and came hacking back towards me at a million miles an hour. Somewhere between the reeds, the gully and my right boot (which he'd hurtled past, missing it by about three inches), we parted company forever. The bigger, darker chub I lost sight of when the lighter one took the fly – and that's the last I saw of either of them. No doubt they're still around somewhere, or at least I like to think they are, perhaps causing havoc amongst the crayfish, and one of them may be just slightly warier of things like black ladybirds dropping into the water.

Night fishing for chub is always great fun. Scott, Dave and I would make frequent evening trips to the stream, fishing on until about one or two in the morning, depending on how things were going. Sometimes, if we were on a bit of a roll, we'd end up staying out until some unearthly hour, even in really terrible weather, in the hope of a few chub. I well remember one such night, fishing a favourite spot of ours on the inside of a deep bend we called The Cave. Dave and I, ever eager, arrived in daylight one winter's evening and set up in our little spot high above the water to await the fish. I think we may even have caught a few. As the evening progressed, we noticed it getting colder and colder, and as the moon rose from behind the trees, bright and full, large as a neon beach ball, we began to wonder firstly, where the chub had gone and secondly, quite what the hell we were doing still sitting there. When we finally decided to pack up at some hour not even invented, the landing net was frozen solid – an elongated rictus of a tennis racket – to the grass. The temperature, and ours along with it, had dropped to minus 6ºC.

Tactics for after dark chubbing were simplicity itself. In my case, the only difference from daylight fishing was that I'd sit in one spot for the duration of the trip instead of chasing imaginary baddies behind trees and bushes. The only addition to the tackle, when the light dropped, was a tiny Betalight inserted in the rod tip so that we could see any indications when a fish picked up the bait. Invariably, baits were big cubes of luncheon meat or the traditional lobworm. With the onset of darkness, finicky fish lost their caution and whereas in the afternoon all we might have experienced would have been niggly little plucks and tweaks, after dark the Betalights in the rod tips would herald great shooting star takes. A preliminary little nudge on the tip would be followed with the fish obviously moving off with the bait and almost dragging the rod in.

The largest chub any of us ever caught from the Rib was one of 4lb 9oz that Dave sneaked out from under my nose just downstream from the bailiff's cottage in Bengeo one night. It was winter, already dark, and I was contentedly sitting in my usual spot casting downstream into the deep corner pool to my right. Then Dave arrived. Starved for company, he sat hard by my side and angled a cast upstream, two or three yards to the left, which must have meant that his bait was sitting in what amounted to six inches of streamy water. Quietly thinking to myself that the chub count at the end of the evening would read something like thirty:nil (in my favour), my lower jaw unhinged somewhat when Dave grabbed for his rod, and with that eternally surprised turn of phrase of his, exclaimed, 'Blimey, I'm in!'

As we looked in the landing net at that beast of a fish, I think we both wondered how on earth it managed to sneak in to the swim, pick up his luncheon meat and fight its way to the net in six inches of water without lying sideways. Or maybe it did lie sideways. Perhaps, with all the excitement, and in that dim light, we hadn't noticed that Dave was the only captor in living memory of a 4lb 9oz River Rib flounder.

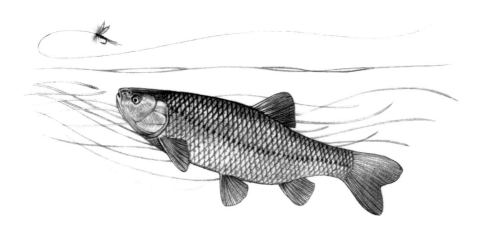

HATS

The fishing hat has always intrigued me. I've always placed great importance on this item of clothing, and the reasoning behind any choice I've made over the years has had nothing to do with practicality. It should have done, but unfortunately it hasn't. Therefore my choice in hats has more often than not left me sitting there with something on my head which hasn't been up to the job for which it was intended. Fool that I am I'll never learn, so what the hell? My good friends, Scotty, Vince and Dave have long since realised that to question my judgement is pointless, and after forty years they woefully sit there wondering why the hell I do it.

During my early teens I always wore what is commonly known as a Greek Fisherman's Hat. John Lennon wore a black one and it looked good on him; no one seemed to question his judgement. Mine were in three colours – black, yellow and white. I used to wear them everywhere, even when I wasn't fishing. Then came the era of the floppy Dick Walker hat, and Vince, Scott and I all went down this sartorial path. My particular hat was the one that regularly and unfortunately ran the gauntlet of the guys in the Greaves & Thomas Angling Society on our monthly club outings on the coach when I was a club junior.

For a number of years I was in the wilderness – Pledger's Head: The Wilderness Years – and wore a variety of fishing hats. If recollection is kind, I suppose their choice did reflect the weather conditions to some extent: wide brims or peaks for when it was sunny, lighter cottons in the summer, heavier materials in the winter, waterproof for when it was raining and so on. And yet… the trouble was, I wasn't happy. None of these hats had the originality I was looking for. I've always been one to disregard whatever everyone else is doing or wearing, so it came to a point where I was fed up with the whole thing and decided a rethink was in order. I needed a new fishing hat, and this led me down a path which, unbeknown to me, would become fraught with the sort of problems that only I, it seems, could have unleashed. There on the path, Pandora's Box lay in front of me and, as usual, I just had to take a peek inside…

Now, the classiest hat I can think of must surely be the one sported by Gene Hackman in that superb 1971 film, *The French Connection*. Hackman played the character Popeye Doyle, a hard-bitten New York cop. In the film he wore his now legendary pork pie hat, and I defy anyone to say that this hat does not ooze class and style. Pork pies are also loved by the old black jazz musicians, so Gene and his hat were always in good company. And, whether or not they'd appreciate it, the angler Maurice Pledger was going to join them. The pork pie had the extra something I needed, insofar as nobody, but nobody, wears a pork pie to go fishing in – such a hat is not waterproof and the brim is so pitifully narrow that it won't shade your eyes on a sunny day. Yet naturally – natch, dude – I'd be wearing my dark glasses anyway, and I'd be looking so phenomenally cool and hip that nobody would dare question the judgement of someone who obviously knew what he was doing. Yes, a Gene Hackman, Popeye Doyle, narrow-brimmed pork pie hat would be my choice.

I let everyone in our little band of friends know, and was of course derided for my pains, but this made me even more determined to get a pork pie. In fact, just to irritate everyone further, I'd get two – one for fishing and one for everyday wear. The decision was made. Now, where to get one? At first I looked on the Internet; in 2004 there were plenty of sites, mostly in America, which advertised and gave details of the fabled hat. I printed out details of the standard measurements, the important one being the width of the brim (1⅝″ – no more, no less).

At the time, being new to all this Internet business, I shied off ordering one sight unseen, as it were. Douglas, my son, seeing my plight, suggested I should visit a reputable hatter's in Jermyn Street in London; Bates, Gentlemen's Hatter. This sounded more to my liking. Off I went. I found the shop, a lovely, traditional, dark and inviting shop seemingly trapped in a time warp. One of two nice old gents approached me – perhaps we were equally trapped in the same time warp – and asked if I needed any help. I showed him photos of *The French Connection* and told him what I was looking for. He nodded knowingly, then took me to a great pile of pork pies and proceeded to take my measurement. He then pulled out a few for me to try. This felt good. This felt very good.

My eyes wandered to a large, glass-fronted case in which sat a massive, stuffed, ginger-and-white cat - wearing a top hat. Binks, as he was called, had adopted the shop back in the nineteen-twenties. He frequented the place until he died, whereupon the owners had him set up so that the clients of the day could remember him. I liked the absurdity and eccentricity of this shop and felt my hat would have the same aura about it. It would feel at home on my head. Perhaps I would call it Binks.

My hat – a black one – was chosen, held above a steaming kettle, expertly brushed and fitted on my head. Perfect. I was in love with it immediately – the only problem being that there was also a brown one, and I didn't know which hat to choose. Out came the brown one. More steaming and expert brushing, more looking up at Binks who looked down glassy eyed and with an air of authority enhanced by the top hat. After deliberating over black or brown like an old woman hovering over eight pairs of shoes, I chose the black one, paid the £75, placed the hat on my head, said goodbye to the man and the cat and walked out the door. Gene Hackman had left the building.

I hadn't gone twenty steps when I looked down to see my feet turn round, face the way I'd just come, and found myself re-entering Bates, Gentlemen's Hatter. Five minutes later, and with another £75 less in my bank account, I said goodbye to the nice man and Binks once again, and walked out into the daylight with the additional brown hat in a bag. The old gentleman's expression, as the cat's, hadn't changed on my second arrival, and this boded well, mistakenly causing me to think that all was well with the world, including all its hats.

As I walked back to the train station I casually glanced at my reflection in shop windows as I passed by. Even though I'd just spent £150 on two hats something wasn't quite right. It wasn't until I was sitting on the train and read again through all the American pork pie measurements that I realised my hat brims looked slightly wider than those illustrated. And once this little niggle had set in, it began to be difficult for me to live with – especially since when I got home I found a tape measure and discovered that the brims were a vast 2″ wide, rather than the de rigueur 1⅝″. Things got much worse when I dropped round to call on Stuart, my daughter's boyfriend. His sister Joanna opened the door.

'Oooh, look! A Jewish hat, you need ringlets…'

That destroyed any idea that Gene Hackman was now living in Hoddesdon, and my prized hats were now semi-prized hats with brims too wide, and most definitely not the ones I'd originally intended.

I phoned Bates, Gentlemen's Hatter and enquired as to what could be done, my mind thinking along the lines of sending them back to have the brims cut back to 1⅝″. Of course, the old gentleman, whose expression had (I'm guessing) finally showed signs of cracking, told me that under no circumstances should be brims be cut back, since it would ruin the felt. I put the phone down, and looking far, far into space, I determined to take the hats somewhere locally to have something done to them – 'something' such as under no circumstances having the brims cut back to 1⅝″. Not knowing much about these kinds of things, I bit the bullet and did the most un-Gene Hackman thing I could imagine, and walked into a little girl's ballet shop in Hoddesdon, where I'd heard they 'did alterations'.

Luckily, no-one other than the pretty young lady behind the counter was present, and she kindly – very, perhaps even suspiciously, kindly – waited for me to retell the whole sorry tale, showing her the photos, printouts and

WHILE MY FLOAT'S STILL COCKED

everything, before telling me she couldn't help. This took twenty minutes. She did, however, point me in the direction of a dry-cleaners owned by a Greek family, who also did alterations – in fact, all kinds of alterations. I was way past the point of embarrassment on this one, having just walked out of a ballet shop, so I set about explaining the whole thing all over again to a bemused Greek lad who kept calling me 'Boss'.

I borrowed his ruler, measured the brim at 2″, and told him it needed to be cut back to 1⅝″. He even wrote the measurement on a small piece of paper and attached it to the brown hat.

'No worries, Boss, I'll get my Mum to do it for you. It will be perfect. Come back Saturday, Boss.'

He said it would cost £3.50 and that he'd get his Mum to do the brown one first.

Saturday arrived. I walked into the shop. I could see the hat hanging up, wrapped in clear polythene, ready for me to collect. The young lad came out as I was opening my wallet.

'Hello, Boss.'

'Oh hello, remember me? I've come for my hat. I see your Mum's finished it.'

'Yes, it's all finished – but you can't have it. You won't like it.'

'Did she manage to do it okay?'

'Oh yes, Boss, it was all fine. All fine. You won't like it.'

'Oh I'm sure I will. She managed to cut it back okay then?'

'Yes, Boss. She managed it fine. But you won't like it.'

By now the broken gramophone record act was starting to wear a little thin, so I tried again.

'Well, I'm sure if she managed to cut it back okay, I'll love it.'

'She cut it back okay, Boss. But you can't have it. You won't like it.'

The wearing-thin wore through and, still trying to keep the puzzlement from invading my face, I asked if I could at least see my £75 hat.

He went over, reached up, got the polythene-wrapped hat down and proceeded to open it. Being one to know the impossibility of turning the clock back, I could see where he was coming from about me 'not liking it'... his dear Mum, bless her poor unknowing Greek soul for never having watched *The French Connection*, had measured 1⅝″ from the outside of the brim inwards, instead of from the inside of the brim outwards. She'd happily cut all the way around it, effectively leaving me with a most wonderful *French Connection* Gene Hackman Fez, whose brim now measured ⅜″ wide. The remaining piece of the 1⅝″ cut-away brim lay loose in the bag like a big circular slice of brown orange peel.

The alternative to waving goodbye to £75 and paying his dear Mum £3.50 for the opportunity of ruining my afternoon was to take up the lad's suggestion of having her stitch it all back on again. This she most certainly did, and I at least have a kind of pork pie with a befitting pedigree, coming as it does from a shop with a stuffed cat in a top hat, passing through a little girl's ballet shop, and ending up being put through a Greek meat slicer, then handed back to me at a price of a mere £7.00 for the extra alteration. I wear it with pride, because apparently...

I am the Boss.

LEVIATHAN, KING'S WEIR*

I know the angler who arrived on my East Bank this afternoon. I have known him for almost forty years, and in that time I have quietly watched his manner and learnt his ways. His humour endeared me to him and I like the way he has treated my fish. Over the many years I have been here, I have been witness to countless anglers, some who have pleased me, while many I have detested greatly, but I find myself at ease when today's visitor comes to fish. I like him.

It is just over an hour past midday now, with perhaps only three hours of remaining fishing light left for him. I see no one else is on the pool. As I say, I am familiar with his manner and his ways, and as he tackled up I knew that he would shortly be casting out a big lobworm and diligently fishing it around the gravels, searching for the fish. Today I noticed he tackled up an old soft-actioned 10′ 8″ Hardy's 1930 cane rod – a mere seventy-four years young – and matched it with his old faithful Mitchell 314 on which is some gossamer 4lb line and a size 6 hook. His enjoyment of things from the past pleases me.

I am glad I had dropped the water level slightly from yesterday; not even my good friend would have managed to fish water that high. Overnight it had lowered a little, still very coloured, but today it was rising. Within two hours it would again be a raging dragon. I knew he relished these conditions so I just settled back to watch.

King's Weir on the River Lea at Turnford in Hertfordshire. Constructed c.1771 during the reign of King George III.

I favoured the current slightly to his advantage, causing a small group of chub to alter position in the pool and seek a more comfortable area in which to lie. As they swung across the current, one of the chub immediately made a grab for the lobworm which he had been quietly inching over the gravel. A lovely deep mid-January fish of 5lb 9oz. I could see the happiness on the face of my friend, the angler, sense the memories the day would give him and the respect he showed my fish. Yes, I liked him a great deal and I liked to help him on occasion.

A little while later, I noticed the lovely old cane gracefully curve into another big chub, one of the first's smaller brothers, weighing 4lb 9oz. A wonderful brace of fish. I saw the angler strike a few times more, then as the waters continued to rise the pool started to change. I think the chub must have felt the push of current was just too much for them, and one by one, they moved out of the pool.

For the next two hours the bites slowed down, but I could see the eagerness on his face was growing. He held the old cane keenly, feeling the line for the slightest bite as he moved the worm around the pool. I was slightly worried that he had to keep moving back his chair every ten minutes as the waters kept rising, but for now he was okay.

He liked my big weir-pool chub – my biggest was a deep-chested, bull-like chub of over seven pounds. He had got the measure of these incredible fish over the years, and perhaps he did not really need my help at all. Just now and then, on a lean day, I would alter the current or swing some streamer weed for him and send a fish his way. In two or three years time he would fall in love with my big perch and I will keep a nice surprise for him, but for now nothing would sway him from his beloved chub. He would not even think of my huge barbel. Perhaps he fished other rivers where these fish would cloud his mind.

I am familiar, of course, with all of the barbel in my pool, some of them fish of twelve and thirteen pounds. I know all their little ways; the places they like to hide during the day; where they will feed. They are all my friends and I can tell at any one time where any one of them will be and what it will be doing. Sometimes, though, we have a visitor, a wanderer from downstream who has come up for a look around the pool. Even I, in times like these, cannot be sure who or just how big the visitor is. It takes time for me to get to know my fish. I watch them grow from tiny fry on the shallows. Many hundreds, thousands, of these fry never survive, but with every day that passes, each fish that manages to see a new dawn, a new dusk, becomes one of my friends. I know their habits and where they will be in times of low water and high. In times of fast rising water such as this, for example, they will be retreating into the quieter corners of the pool and under the sill. Now and then, on a very rare day indeed, a stranger may drift into my pool unannounced, marauding silently over the gravels. No one sees. The fish that were just about holding station a few hours ago have been slowly forced out in ones and twos by the increasing current, and now they have gone.

Water clarity is now down to two or three inches at most. Even the largest stones are being bounced along the bottom, finding purchase against a trapped branch which in turn is uplifted by the increasing strain of other accumulating debris. The tail of a tiny bullhead, hunkered down, wavers from underneath another scuttling stone as the mailed flank of this unseen visitor brushes past into the pool. I cannot make out his size, but for certain he is a barbel, and from the fleeting glimpse of his flank and of how he is

pushing through the flow, he is of an uncommon size.

Above the pool, daylight is all but gone. I can see my friend look at his timepiece; it is close to five bells and he has already made his last cast while I was taken with looking for the new fish. The lights have been switched on in the lock house, and as he looks across the deafening cauldron of water now spilling over the sill, he sees that it is backlit and level with the brickwork. The waves, heaving and pulsing irresistibly down the centre of the pool, crashing continually in a terrifying halo of light, must be nearly three feet high. The water-level is rising at an alarming rate, and I fear my angler must beat a retreat before he is cut off entirely. I happen to look over to him, just as he appears to be questioning the tautness in the line over his finger.

The old Hardy sweeps over his shoulder; the tip of the rod more or less stays where it is. He has reacted to a solid thump on two huge lobworms which he had just placed under the trailing branches of the old willow to his left. He is on his feet now, and I can tell from his manner that he is unsure of what he has hooked. The seventy-four-year-old cane is in a full hoop, yet even with 4lb line, the softness of the rod can allow him to effect some degree of pull on the fish. He is still uncertain, I can tell. He winds down a few times, lifts the rod and there is just a heavy yawing of the split-cane tip. I know that ridiculous things start to go through his mind:

'This is a fish. I felt a savage bite. Is this a fish? Is this a tree? A rock? A living rock?'

Within two seconds the jumble of thoughts is unravelled as fast as his line. I know. His adversary, now realising that he has to deal with this new irritation as well as a raging weir pool, heads off towards open water and the sill. How could any living creature possibly head off into the mayhem of open water against that current? It is irresistible. It is impossible. Even my friend, with the rod angled low, trying to off-balance the fish, has to fight it. It just keeps on – and on.

It kept on, the torrent of current. Suddenly the fish turned towards the bank and the angler gained some lost line, but in doing so the fish hit a contra-flow, a massive back-eddy, which in effect now helped him gain momentum again and power off once more, this time with an awful dragging current at his back. The water was still rising quickly, well up the path, and was now rushing back along it, creating what was almost a new river behind a ridge of high ground and a stand of trees overhanging the pool.

The fish was now in the bay in front of the next swim along, effectively downstream because of these ever changing currents. The angler could no longer play it out from where he was, and his only option was to somehow move into the next swim along. It was as dark as pitch now. The only light – from the lock-house on the opposite bank of the pool – was too far away to be of any help to him. In order for him to move into the next swim, he had to pass the rod around several trees while negotiating gushing water, water roaring below his feet, slipping and cracking branches, twigs flinging back in his face. There was no real hope in his heart for anything; he had no real plan. Whatever else he found himself doing, he just kept the rod in his hand somehow, criss-crossing it round tree trunks and branches, with the line catching each and every twig, pinging free and then catching again. He concentrated on keeping the fish on a taut line. He concentrated on not falling in. He tried not to think of the possibility of drowning.

It was a full five minutes before he made it to the other side. Breathless, he started to reel in the line. The area in front of him was a large circular bay in which the current was forcefully sucked back up towards the sill, with seemingly just as much power as that which was cannonading past in the other direction, where the force of the river ran on the other side of a narrow line of willows growing out in the pool. These willows, with their entanglement of branches and roots, were being laid sideways by the dragon, rising, juddering and submerging on their unstable platform below on a gravel spit that was probably being torn apart.

Turn by turn, the old Mitchell slowly retrieved the drowned line. The unseen monster had used his time wisely, and had headed straight for the willows, as my friend imagined he would. With every turn of the reel, his hopes rose. Expecting everything to lock up solidly at any moment, he was surprised beyond words to feel the fish still on a free line clear of the trees, and coming towards him.

For the first time in half an hour he felt that maybe he could land this fish. Surely, after all this, now his prize was in open water in front of him, and if he could only keep him there, quietly without panicking, he could just glide him into the net.

Everything was closing in on him – the night, the trees, the thunderous noise from the weir, the sight of the waves crashing down in the main pool, – being attached to a living fish of unknown size, immense size, on such frail tackle… it quite simply frightened him. Just what would meet his gaze when he got this fish to turn over on the surface?

He was now actually scared.

The cane lurched over and the fish nose-dived to the bottom. For five minutes, nothing he could do could lift it again. The rod stayed in one place, nodding quietly, while down below the barbel calmly held station in one spot in a current that would have had trees float by. He could feel his head slowly moving from side to side, and knew the fish wasn't foul-hooked in any way. Without warning it turned its back to the current and tore off along the right-hand side of the bay. Here was a long, tangled line of trees and submerged roots which eventually curved round to join the willows out on the spit. Line screamed off the Mitchell. The fish must have reached some limit of clear water; it edged off and allowed itself to be slowly drawn back to the centre of the bay. Again he brought the fish into mid water, just below the rod tip, where it would hang in the current. Several times it turned and powered off and was brought back to exactly the same spot. Nothing the angler could do could lift it the final two or three feet needed to enable him to get it to the surface, and then hopefully use the current to simply let it float into the waiting net.

In the confined blackness of the bay there wasn't enough light to see what he was doing, and in any case he couldn't hold a net ready in the ferocious water – not for that kind of netting.

He needed a torch.

Fumbling in his pocket he realised the torch was back with his chair at the other swim. He tried once again to draw the fish to the surface but it was hopeless. There was no strength left in his arm, no strength left in the rod and none in the line, not even with guesswork added. He needed that torch. The only thing he could do was lay the rod down on the ground, open the bail arm on the Mitchell, and run back to get it.

One chance.

As he ran back to get the torch, the big fish took his own chance. In the thirty seconds it took for the angler to return the fish had swum straight back to the willows. He clicked over the bail arm and began to wind in. He knew where the fish had gone, imagined it would go there, and wasn't surprised in the least. He smiled at its cunning, admired its move. As the cane curled over he could feel the satisfying pull of a heavy sullen weight on a free line, but it was impossibly close to all those willow roots.

A second later there was a moment, the only moment since his bait had been picked up, that he felt the life go from the line, then an instant later, catch again on a snag. The fish had gone.

In that instant he was nine years old again, standing in the little brook at the bottom of his garden with his minnow net. His prized dace, balanced perfectly half-in, half-out on the rim of the net.

That same split second where it all falls away…

Over forty years ago it mattered dreadfully, but this time it didn't. He knew this fish had gone. For ten minutes he hand lined and pulled, let the line go slack, tried everything he knew just in case he'd imagined that awful moment, thinking he was wrong. But with every moment that passed he just smiled – and then smiled even more. It had been an hour since his lobworm had been picked up under that willow.

He knew in the end he'd have to pull for a break, but it didn't matter. It didn't matter at all, because his fish had gone, and more importantly, he knew his hook was just stuck in a tree.

The line gave on his final pull, and he wound it back onto the beloved Mitchell. He smiled and laughed. He thanked his rod, thanked his reel, thanked the fish and wished him well. He admired and saluted the grandest fight of his life with the grandest fish of his life: a fish of unknown size, most certainly a barbel and most certainly equal to the dace in the little brook at the bottom of his garden all those years ago.

The more he thought about it, the more he was pleased – even pleased that he'd lost that fish, because there would be plenty of others to catch on other days.

That fish really did deserve to get away, and maybe it could be argued that I helped him a little, who knows. What counts is that my friend will now go home happy, with a memory that will stay with him forever. I too am happy, and pleased for him, and if he does feel a little saddened by the loss, then in the small way of return perhaps – yes very possibly, even definitely – I shall favour him with a special perch in a few years' time.

JUST ONE MORE CAST

...And so here we are. The red-tipped float has been inched down the glide and is finally drifting towards the tail of the swim. We hold it back a while, in the anticipation that a large roach or the perch of our dreams takes hold, but whether it does or not, it doesn't really matter. The float has travelled the course of the stream, gently creasing the ripples, idly passing clucking moorhens and being brushed narrowly and askance by a kingfisher whirling past, arrow-straight, on its journey downstream. Little instances of time gather like small rafts of leaves, momentarily nestling against trailing willow fronds, sometimes rushing by, sometimes lingering lazily, then catching the relentless drift again and moving on. Memories come and go under heavy-lidded eyes, of remembered friends, of times gone by, a gentle smile at recollections maybe never to return. This, then, is our float. It's ours to use while we are here, searching the water, carrying the bait to our fish, summoning spirits of kindly anglers long since passed to return and sit with us as we enjoy once again the love we all share, which is simply called 'fishing.'

Perhaps you will find something in these pages that will stir your memory, cause you to shed a tear, or to chuckle at a happy recollection from the distant past. Then, if you are tempted to return to a favourite swim, and maybe to sit awhile and reflect with fondness on times gone by, then I would say that it has all been well worthwhile – to share your company and to write down a few of my own angling memories... *while my float's still cocked.*

Zander – a future candidate for the the sixpence jar?

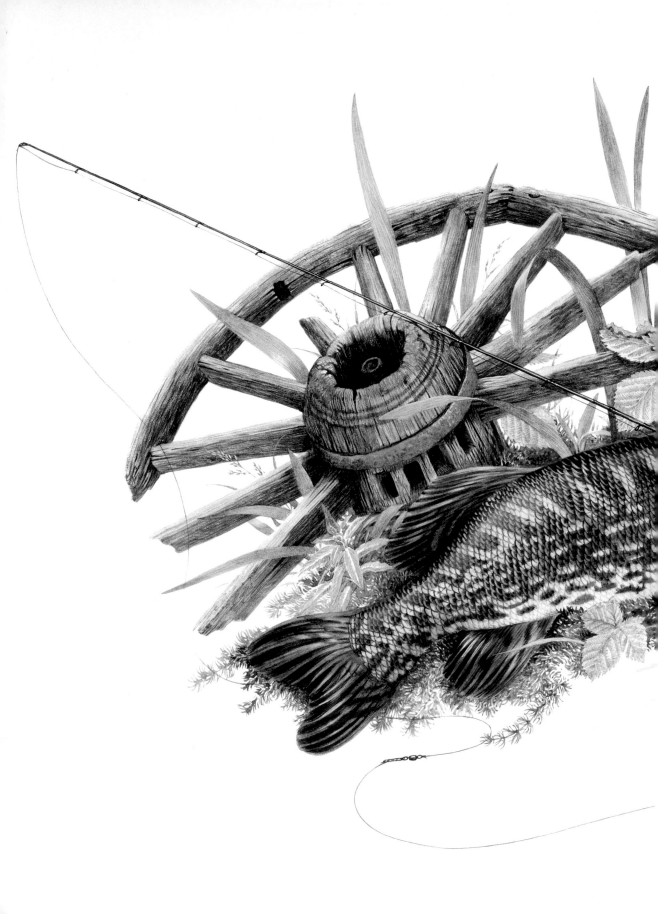